A Short History of Reno

A Short History of Reno

A Short History of Reno

Barbara and Myrick Land

University of Nevada Press
RENO LAS VEGAS

The authors wish to thank Michael Witter, editor and publisher at
Lexikos (San Francisco), for working with them on this project and
taking it through the editing and typesetting stages.

The paper used in this book meets the requirements of American
National Standard for Information Sciences—Permanence of Paper
for Printed Library Materials, ANSI Z39.48-1984. Binding materials
were selected for strength and durability.

Library of Congress Cataloging-in-Publication Data
Land, Barbara.
   A short history of Reno / Barbara N. Land and Myrick E. Land.
      p.   cm.
   Includes index.
   ISBN 0-87417-262-4 (pbk. : acid-free paper)
   1. Reno (Nev.)—History.   I. Land, Myrick, 1922– . II. Title.
F849.R4L35   1995
979.3'55—dc20   94-32428
                                        CIP

University of Nevada Press, Reno, Nevada 89557 USA
12   11   10   09   08   07   7   6   5   4

ISBN-13: 978-0-87417-262-1 (pbk. : alk. paper)

A Thousand Thanks. . .

We've learned a lot about Reno from many generous Nevadans who lived here before we came. Much of the background for this book was provided by helpful librarians at:

The Nevada Historical Society
Getchell Library, University of Nevada, Reno
Oral History Program, University of Nevada, Reno
Washoe County Libraries
Reno Gazette-Journal

Personal reminiscences and clues to sources came from dozens of Reno people. We're especially grateful to Robert and Joyce Laxalt who read the whole manuscript. For more stories and advice, we thank Bill Berry, Helen Blue, Lloyd Boles, Mark Curtis, Ann Dalbec, Don Dondero, Jim Ellis, Philip Earl, Martha Filipas, Bill Henricks, Jake Highton, James Hulse, Carole Keith, Tom King, Warren and Janet Lerude, Rollan and Marilyn Melton, Caroline Morel, Lee Mortensen, Stanley Paher, Nita Philips and Linda Sommer.

To our friends in
The Biggest Little City

Contents

1   Road to Riches   page 5

2   The Comstock Connection   page 19

3   Birth of Sin City   page 33

4   Matrimonial Games   page 45

5   Millionaires and Movie Stars   page 59

6   Politics, Nevada Style   page 71

7   Strangers Who Changed a City   page 85

8   Breaking Through the Red Line   page 101

9   Biggest Little City   page 115

Selected Bibliography   page 126

Index   page 128

Road to Riches

1

Two sisters from Forks, Washington, got off the bus in Reno one windy spring day and headed for Harrah's Casino. Like the seven million other visitors who swarm into the Reno-Lake Tahoe area every year, Mary Reynolds and Frankie Kennedy hoped to go home richer—a little or a lot—after hitting a big jackpot or picking the lucky numbers.

They might lose, of course, but they promised each other they'd risk no more than the money they had saved to gamble during this brief vacation.

"My husband would never let me hear the end of it if I came home with an empty purse," said Reynolds. So the two women were cautious. But when they saw the bank of one-dollar slot machines with a "Megabucks" sign announcing a three-million-dollar jackpot, they looked at each other and said, "Why not?"

Pooling their cash, they bought a roll of silver-dollar tokens. Kennedy urged Reynolds to insert the coins and pull the handle. One by one, or three at a time, dollars disappeared into the slot. No bells. No colored lights. No return of dollars.

As she deposited the last three tokens into the machine, Reynolds shrugged and picked up her purse, ready to quit. Then bells began to ring as four sevens lined up. Somebody said, "You've won 3.2 million dollars!"

Kennedy and Reynolds hugged each other as a crowd gathered and Harrah's executives hurried over to confirm the winning jackpot. The winners rushed off to the VIP office to phone home.

"He'll never believe this!" Reynolds said as she excitedly dialed her husband's number. She was right. He didn't believe her. Just laughed and said, "Do you think I don't know what day this is?"

Opposite page
Horsedrawn wagons clattered through downtown Reno in the 1890s, joining the bustling traffic in front of the Palace Hotel.

In all the excitement, the two sisters had forgotten the date—April Fools' Day. But the jackpot was real.

Native Gamblers: Reno has been a gambler's town from the beginning. Even Native Americans—Washoe, Paiute and Shoshone tribes who camped along the Truckee River long before there was a town called Reno—liked to bet on games and contests when they celebrated a rabbit hunt or pine-nut harvest.

"Their wagers," according to Nevada historian Russell Elliott, "involved baskets, leathers, jewelry, buckskins, and prized rabbit-skin blankets."

For the Washoes, Paiutes and Shoshones who passed through the area, games were a celebration—a welcome break in their endless search for food. They moved with the seasons, hunting rabbits and ground squirrels in the desert, fishing in the rivers and lakes, climbing into the high country for deer and mountain sheep.

A bear was the ultimate prize. A Washoe brave who killed a bear and shared the meat with his fellow wanderers was a hero. The bear's skin was his to keep. When he wore it, he believed the bear skin gave him magic powers, strength and wisdom.

If a single rabbit seemed insignificant by comparison with a bear, a whole blanket made of rabbit skins was another matter. Washoes recognized a bear skin as the cloak of a wise man. Only a rich man could keep warm in a rabbit skin blanket.

Reno had no glittery casinos in 1907, but any street-corner game of chance could attract a crowd.

"Permanent homes were out of the question," Elliott wrote, "for a people whose economy forced them to . . . scour the land for a livelihood."

They didn't plant crops in those days, but they knew the habits of migratory birds, knew where to look for fish, understood the ways of small animals who could be lured out of their burrows. In summer, bands of Indians roamed the mountains and meadows, setting up temporary villages of grass-covered tipis. In winter they moved to sheltered valleys where they sometimes dug foundations for sturdier structures of branches and bark.

Before the first snows, they gathered and stored wild grains and seeds and desert grasses to be used for bread and soup during the winter. Pine nuts, from the piñon pine, were a staple and the pine nut harvest was a time for family reunions. The celebration included everybody, from revered elders to babies in back pouches.

At the first frost, families and friends gathered in the piñon groves. They knew the trees would be waiting with pine cones full of seeds. Men carried willow poles to beat the cones out of the trees. Women collected them in deep baskets strapped to their foreheads.

After the nuts were gathered, shelled, cleaned and roasted, it was time for fun and games. The men would flex their muscles, bring out their treasures and place bets on the strongest or swiftest braves in a series of contests.

Even now, in Washoe country, the pine nut harvest is a yearly event, no longer reserved for Native Americans who remember the old ways. Nevadans whose ethnic origins may be Italian, Basque, Chinese, German or English like to hunt for pine nuts in early fall. It's a happy excuse for a family hike and picnic in the woods. Later, the nuts they find will turn up in cookies, salads, stews and sauces.

Commercial packagers now harvest the nuts and sell them as delicacies. Visitors to Reno find pine nut ice cream on restaurant menus.

Trappers and Mapmakers: For centuries, native tribes had the place to themselves. As late as 1776, when Spanish explorers were blazing their westward trails some 500 miles to the south, no white man had ventured into the region the Spanish called the "Northern Mystery." When white men discovered the green oasis, early in the 19th century, "luck" became an everyday word in the Truckee Meadows.

Jedediah Smith, a trapper for the Rocky Mountain Fur Company, hoped to find a fortune in beaver skins along the river in 1827—but the beavers

The Paiute Hand Game: This was a gambling sport in which the Indians often bet everything they owned—their blankets, baskets and their beads. The game often lasted four or five days without stopping; as one game was finished the next one started. When the players grew tired, they simply got up and moved a few feet away into the brush to sleep, letting others take their places.
—*Survival Arts of the Primitive Paiutes* by Margaret M. Wheat

Reno artist Robert Caples painted the desert landscape and sketched this Indian tribal chief in his feathered headdress.

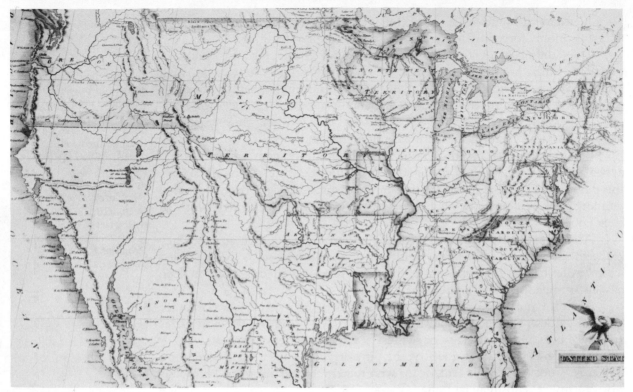

In 1823, maps of the United States showed miles of unexplored territory in the west. This cartographer drew in the mythical Buenaventura River, connecting the Pacific and the Rockies.

disappeared into safer waters. Bad luck for Smith. Still, he did meet some friendly Paiutes and opened the way for later explorers.

When John C. Frémont, pathfinder for the U.S. Army Topographical Engineers, led an 1844 expedition through the Black Rock Desert to Pyramid Lake and the Truckee River, he was searching for the Buenaventura River, a mythical water highway from the Rocky Mountains to the Pacific Ocean.

Frémont knew the swift little river that fed Pyramid Lake wasn't big enough to be the Buenaventura, but it was full of fish—enough for several banquets for himself and his desert-weary men. By this time, he suspected the Buenaventura River didn't exist. Perhaps it was simply the creation of an imaginative mapmaker. But these fish were real—a lucky discovery.

The explorer called the fish "salmon trout," because of their pink meat, and named the clear mountain stream the Salmon Trout River. Later mapmakers changed the name to the Truckee River, honoring a Paiute chief who helped them find their way through the wilderness.

Winter of Hunger: Two years after Frémont's 1844 mapping expedition, a wagon train of emigrants thought their troubles were over when they came upon the Truckee Meadows in October 1846. These were families on their way to the Promised Land beyond the Sierra Nevada. Exhausted after grueling weeks of desert heat and hardship, they welcomed the sparkling river and cool shade.

Nobody was more relieved than their leader, the patriarchal George Donner. He and his family had left Springfield, Illinois, in April to join other wagons for the trip west from Missouri. By July the whole train had reached Wyoming and was about to proceed along the tested and recommended Oregon Trail. But George Donner and his older brother, Jake, were impatient .

They had read *The Emigrants Guide to Oregon and California,* a new book by Lansford Hastings, a young adventurer who said he had found a short cut on a return trip from California. The route through Utah, he said, was much faster than the prescribed Oregon route. So the Donner brothers persuaded some of the families to leave the rest of the wagon train and follow Hastings's short cut.

The new route may have been quicker for Hastings, one man on horseback, but clumsy wagons couldn't travel so easily over mountains. Twenty wagonloads of men, women and children were running out of food and water. They sent two scouts ahead to Sutter's Fort in California to try to bring back supplies.

In the Truckee Meadows their hopes revived. Even though it was late October and they had been warned to cross the Sierra before heavy snows covered the trails, they agreed to rest for a few days in this pleasant campground. It was a fatal mistake. When they reached the mountain pass later known as Donner Pass, on the last day of October, heavy snows forced them to turn back.

On the shores of a frozen lake—now Donner Lake—they set up camp. Through a winter of starvation and death they struggled to stay alive long enough to continue their journey west. Only half of their number survived.

The tragic story of the Donner Party has been told and retold, based on first-hand accounts by the few survivors and on diaries and letters left behind. Most often repeated are gruesome accounts of cannibalism. When their supplies ran out, the stranded families ate whatever they could find—cattle frozen in the snow, boiled leather shoes, wagon harness. When old people and babies starved to death, they, too, were eaten.

In midwinter, a party of seventeen men and women left the camp and

Explorer John C. Frémont led a team of U.S. Army Topographical Engineers who mapped the Great Basin and made the first scientific studies of the region.

"The appearance of the country is so forbidding that I was afraid to enter it."
—John C. Frémont, 1843

"It is such a fascinating land. For all its hardship, I shall hate to leave it."
—John C. Frémont, 1844

attempted to get across the mountains. After thirty-two days of horror, only seven people stumbled into a ranch on the Bear River in California. Ten had died along the way.

The fate of the Donner Party didn't discourage later pioneers from following their trail across the mountains—especially after 1848 when gold was discovered in California. Prospectors from the east, feeling lucky, paused at the green oasis beside the Truckee before crossing the mountains that separated them from fortunes they hoped to find.

As more covered wagons rolled through, the Truckee Meadows became a crossroads where the east-west emigrant trail met the north-south route. If the swift little Truckee River was low, travelers considered themselves lucky. Men and horses didn't have to swim, but could wade across to the other side.

Bridge to Eldorado: They had no other choice—until 1857 when two enterprising settlers, Charles Gates and John F. Stone, built a crude bridge across the river. It didn't last long. Spring floods washed the bridge away and the river became an obstacle once more—until Charles W. Fuller, a settler from Missouri, gambled on travelers' impatience to get across the river and stay dry.

In 1859, Fuller built a log bridge across the Truckee and charged a small fee to anyone who crossed it. He also built a log shelter where tired and dusty prospectors could rest, play cards and exchange news with other gold-seekers. They called the place Fuller's Crossing.

By this time, the first rivers of gold had dried up in California. Still, prospectors continued to arrive in the Truckee Meadows, pursuing rumors that gold had been found in mountains just 20 miles away. The "Rush to Washoe" had begun.

When the first Pony Express riders headed west from St. Joseph, Missouri, in 1860, they passed through Mormon Station, some 35 miles south of the Truckee Meadows, before crossing the Sierra into California. Other adventurous horsemen discovered a pleasant rest stop at Fuller's Crossing. Nothing fancy, but shade trees and cool breezes were a relief after weeks of relentless heat in the desert. Snow-topped mountains in the distance gave riders a hint of the rugged terrain that lay between them and Sacramento.

Fuller's bridge made the trip easier—until the river rose again and demolished the supports. Fuller's luck seemed about to run out. Behind his back, critics of the bridge called it Fuller's Folly, but the Missourian was determined

Myron Lake had a vision of railroads passing through the Truckee Meadows, linking the east and west coasts.

A Short History of Reno

to try again. He rebuilt the bridge in the spring of 1861, then looked around for a chance to quit the toll-bridge business. It was time to try his luck somewhere else.

The man who bought the bridge from Fuller in 1861 hit the jackpot. Myron C. Lake took one look at traffic in the Truckee Meadows and saw visions of the future. This rustic little bridge could become much more than a convenient way to cross the Truckee River.

Some day, Lake believed, railroads would cross this wild country, linking east and west. If the railroad-builders followed routes favored by the Pony Express, they'd have to pass through the Truckee Meadows.

A veteran of the war with Mexico, Lake kept himself informed about military and political developments in Washington. Civil War had been inevitable after South Carolina seceded from the Union in December 1860. When other southern states followed and the Confederacy declared itself a separate nation, President Abraham Lincoln needed help from the West.

From the beginning, Myron Lake made money from his bridge. Tolls were posted:
Horse and Buggy, 50¢
Horses & Buggy, 75¢
Loaded Wagon, $1
Unloaded wagon, 50¢
Footmen, 10¢
Cattle, 6-1/2¢
Horses, 12-1/2¢
Pigs and sheep, 3¢
Additional spans of animals, 50¢

"Lake's bridge and its lucrative tolls always raised Reno's hackles," John M. Townley wrote in *Tough Little Town on the Truckee*. "Although shrouded in pious calls for public ownership, the antagonism was personal, since Lake gave free passage to town residents, afoot or by wagon . . . ."

New Star in the Flag: The discovery of the Comstock Lode in 1859 had brought a flood of gold and silver seekers to the untamed country east of the Sierra. In Washington, President James Buchanan encouraged the United States Congress to divide the huge Utah Territory and

Lake Mansion, at the corner of Virginia Street and California Avenue when this photograph was taken in 1904, was later moved south to Kietzke and Virginia, where it is still preserved as a small museum.

On October 31, 1864, newspaperman Alf Doten noted in his diary: "We got a telegram this morning announcing that the President has issued a proclamation making us a state. Hurrah for the State of Nevada!"

create another future state. Before leaving office in 1861, he signed the Nevada Territory Bill.

Soon after Abraham Lincoln's inauguration, March 4, 1861, the new president appointed a governor for the Territory of Nevada, choosing a loyal Union politician. The day General James Warren Nye arrived in the territorial capital, July 8, 1861, he delivered a rousing speech designed to rally Nevadans to the Union cause.

"Allow me to assure you," he told the Carson City crowd, "that not one star shall be permitted to be removed from the old thirty-four. Twenty-five million free men will not permit it. And I have come to this distant country with the hope of adding one more—a bright and glorious star—Nevada."

The governor kept his promise. Within three years Nevada had become a state.

If Myron Lake heard Nye's first speech as governor, he surely joined in the applause. If he didn't, he could have read about it in the *Territorial Enterprise*. That lively newspaper, printed weekly in Virginia City, brought news of prosperous mining in the Comstock to eager readers in Carson City and the Truckee Meadows. Lake's bridge was a distribution point for the paper.

Soon after he bought Fuller's log bridge, Lake built a stronger one, moving it upstream where natural outcroppings of rock offered better support. Travelers who crossed the bridge needed a shelter, so Lake built an inn. Men on horseback were accustomed to camping under the stars, but one night in a comfortable bed at Lake House was worth a dollar. For another fifty cents a traveler could buy a hot meal at Lake's tavern.

Every horse and driver paid fifty cents to cross Lake's bridge. Every wagon brought him another dollar.

Another Rush to Washoe: The California gold rush had tapered off by 1861, but the Comstock silver rush had just begun—and the only road to Virginia City went right across the new bridge. Supplies for the miners had to cross the bridge. When miners wanted steaks, beef cattle walked across. Lake charged the cattlemen a dollar for each animal. The money poured in.

Lake didn't squander his money or hoard it. Gradually he bought more land and constructed more buildings. Within a year after taking over Fuller's bridge, he also owned a grist mill, a livery stable, and a kiln. Soon after the Homestead Act was passed in 1862 he moved into neighboring rangelands and started raising cattle. Lake's Crossing became a thriving community—and the man who owned so much of it was eager to put it on the map.

Telegraph lines between Sacramento and Salt Lake City replaced Pony Express riders, but the traffic at Lake's Crossing grew heavier. Wagonloads of silver ore came down from Virginia City, bound for the Pacific port of San Francisco. Immigrant farmers, headed for California, came in from the east. Some found Nevada too pleasant to leave, so they settled in the Truckee Meadows and the Carson Valley.

Lake dreamed of a railroad connecting the Atlantic and Pacific coasts—and he was not alone. By 1862, President Lincoln had signed a bill providing for a railroad to be built between Sacramento, California, and Council Bluffs, Iowa. It wasn't going to be easy to lay metal rails through the rugged Sierra Nevada, but a few rich and powerful men believed it could be done.

Charles Crocker, Leland Sanford, Mark Hopkins and Colin Huntington of California organized the Central Pacific Railroad Company and raised funds for the western portion of the Transcontinental Railroad. The eastern portion would be built by the Union Pacific Company, heading west from Omaha, Nebraska. Eventually the two segments would be joined in Utah—

Pony Express riders carried the mail from coast to coast for just a few months—from April 1860 to October 1861 —but they opened a path for later communications companies.

Central Pacific workers laid tracks across Nevada in 1867 and 1868 to complete the western link of the first transcontinental railroad.

but not right away.

Progress was slow. Although the Central Pacific started from Sacramento in the fall of 1863, it would take four years for the rails to reach Nevada. Heavy equipment had to travel by ship from the east to California, and construction costs weren't cheap. Until the Civil War ended in 1865, military expenses drained the Union treasury. Railroads had to wait.

Meanwhile, the big, sparsely-populated Territory of Nevada had become a full-fledged state by October 31, 1864. Nevada volunteers were called into the Union Army and taxes were collected from Nevada citizens to help pay for the war. Some of them had grown very rich from their mining interests in the Comstock.

When the war was over, Myron Lake watched for signs of resumed building on the Central Pacific. Hundreds of Chinese laborers had been recruited for the job and the tracks were growing longer every day. When the steel rails crossed Nevada, Lake wanted to be sure the chosen path included Lake's Crossing.

Not waiting for Fate to settle the question, Lake wrote to Charles Crocker. If the Central Pacific wanted a ready-made town in an ideal location, in a green valley at the foot of the Comstock, Lake could offer the railroad four hundred acres to develop. All he wanted from Crocker was a promise to build a depot on the property.

Before long the two ambitious men were informal partners in a plan to build a city. When the railroad reached the Nevada state line on December 13, 1867, Lake was ready to celebrate. The rails had crossed the mountains, but winter snows made further progress impossible until spring. Lake had to wait four more months until the first locomotive steamed into Lake's Crossing. While waiting, he and Crocker had worked out a specific agreement.

In March 1868, Lake deeded 400 acres to Crocker, who had the land surveyed and divided into lots. The railroad agreed to build its depot at Lake's Crossing and to auction the lots to home builders.

Crocker showed his gratitude by giving 127 lots back to Lake.

W hat's in a Name? The new town would have a new name. Eventually, Crocker believed, it would be the largest city between California and Missouri. Of course, it would also be the junction for the Virginia and Truckee Railroad and the transcontinental line.

What name would be most appropriate for this bustling future city? At first the railroad men considered Argenta, recognizing that silver was the source of the city's wealth. But Crocker preferred to honor an old friend, Civil War General Jesse Lee Reno.

The general's name, anglicized from the French "Renault," was easy to say, to spell and to remember. The general himself had been killed on a Maryland battlefield. Crocker was determined to give the man this tribute. Besides, he felt "Reno" had a certain ring to it.

Comstock miners read about the new town in the *Gold Hill Daily News*. Editors there had favored "Argenta" as a name, but conceded: "Reno is more easily written and the Railroad officials had sense enough to omit 'City,' a term which is usually a burlesque."

The *Carson City Appeal* announced, "Reno has sprung up feathered and lively. We must not let the new city on the Truckee run away with the capitol

Myron Lake's critics included the Reno *Crescent*. On January 21, 1871, the editor wrote: "It becomes us, on bended knee and with bowed heads, to thank God that he has given us such powerful guardian angels to watch over and protect us against the machinations of that wolf in sheep's clothing, M. C. Lake, who ever stands ready to gobble up unwary innocents."

"No one is idle except the man who is too lazy to work," the Reno *Gazette* commented on November 24, 1899. "Altogether we should be—and we are—happy, for we are righteous."

one of these days."

As far away as San Francisco, newspapers reported the opening of the new railroad town. One announcement declared:

R E N O !
VIRGINIA STATION,
— ON THE —
PACIFIC RAILROAD!

AUCTION SALE OF TOWN LOTS

— IN —

THIS NEWLY LOCATED TOWN

WILL TAKE PLACE ON

SATURDAY, MAY 9, 1868.

Beneath this multi-banked headline, the announcement continued:

THIS SALE WILL AFFORD A GRAND OPPORTUNITY for favorable investments in town lots suitable for all kinds of business and trades. The depot being permanently located at this point will give the town of RENO a commanding position of vast importance to secure the trade of Nevada and that portion of California lying east of the Sierras, and will be the natural market for the produce of the rich agricultural valleys north. Situated on the Truckee River, affording water power unsurpassed in the United States, and where the VIRGINIA AND TRUCKEE railroad connects with the PACIFIC, it is unnecessary to enumerate the many advantages this town will possess as the center of immense milling and manufacturing operations.

Of course, it was "unnecessary to enumerate" the advantages. Everybody in the Truckee Meadows knew where most of the town's wealth was coming from. The rich Comstock Lode was just 20 miles away, on the grey slopes of Mount Davidson, and carloads of silver ore were arriving daily now, bound for assay offices in California.

The busy little Virginia and Truckee Railroad brought the ore from Virginia City to "End of the Line"—the only name for the Truckee Meadows settlement until it was officially christened Reno. Now the town was an important stop on the cross-continental Central Pacific Railroad, a vital link between Virginia City and the rest of the world.

The prophets didn't need supernatural powers to predict a prosperous future for Reno. But when it came, that prosperity was unlike anything Myron Lake or Charles Crocker had imagined—and it long outlasted the Comstock Bonanza.

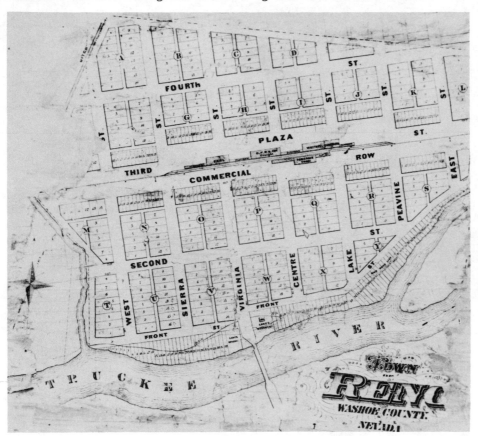

Even before Reno had a name, Charles Crocker had the land surveyed and divided into lots under this first town plan, 1868.

"Reno is in the Great Basin of America, between the Rockies and the Sierra, where the vigor of the sun and the heights of the mountains, to say nothing of the demanding activities of the mining booms, have created a latter day race of tree worshipers."
—*The City of Trembling Leaves*, by Walter Van Tilburg Clark.

The Comstock Connection

2

A skinny young man wearing dusty work boots strolled down the wooden sidewalk of C Street in Virginia City one September day in 1862, six years before Reno was named. He mingled with a crowd of scruffy miners and muleskinners, ambling past five saloons and a feed store.

Saloons were numerous in the bustling town, the young man observed. A bar, he'd heard, was the first commercial enterprise in the primitive mining camp that had become Virginia City. That early saloon was simply two planks supported by whiskey kegs, sheltered from the desert sun by a sheet of canvas. Now the town had a whole string of wooden buildings housing all sorts of businesses.

Just three years after the discovery of rich veins of silver on the slopes of Mount Davidson, here was a busy little metropolis with cigar stores, fruit markets, restaurants, barbershops, bakeries, boarding houses, a hotel—and 25 saloons.

Walking faster now, 25-year-old Sam Clemens strode toward the offices of the *Territorial Enterprise*, the lively newspaper being quoted in San Francisco and New York as the authentic voice of the frontier. Clemens was eager to meet Joe Goodman, the poet-editor who had hired him without meeting him.

Clemens had come west from Missouri where he had worked as a pilot on Mississippi riverboats—until the Civil War halted commercial traffic on the river—then joined the Marion Rangers, a Confederate militia.

A month in the military was enough. When Sam's older brother, Orion Clemens, was appointed Secretary of the new Nevada Territory, young Sam asked to tag along. Orion and his family would be living in Carson City, the

Opposite page
Pistol-packing Wells, Fargo agents in Reno were ready to protect shipments of Comstock gold and silver from train robbers.

territorial capital, but Sam intended to find a fortune in the gold and silver diggings of the West. Everybody knew it was there for the taking.

For nearly a year he pursued riches—but never quite found them—in the gold mines of Aurora, California. Whenever he could get a copy of the *Territorial Enterprise*, he caught up with happenings in Nevada, keeping an alert eye on the mining reports.

The *Enterprise*, arriving by stagecoach from Nevada, kept Aurora miners informed about the excitement in Virginia City. Clemens liked the paper—especially the brash, exaggerated style of Dan De Quille (William Wright), whose ribald humor seemed to match his own. He respected the highly literate Rollin Daggett and the tough, aggressive reporters who seemed to know something about geology and mineralogy.

In the spring of 1862, Clemens started sending the *Enterprise* a few of his own frontier sketches—signing them simply, "Josh." Goodman printed them and asked for more. That summer, he offered "Josh" a job.

Soon after Clemens arrived to accept Goodman's offer, *Enterprise* readers were quoting Josh and looking for his stories in the paper. On Groundhog Day 1863, they discovered a new by-line—one that was to outshine and outlast all other *Enterprise* by-lines. Sam Clemens—Josh—had become "Mark Twain."

The name was a navigation term used on Mississippi riverboats, but to future readers around the world, Mark Twain came to mean lively stories by a truly original American author.

In *Roughing It*, a highly embroidered account of his five years of adventure in California and Nevada, Mark Twain described Virginia City as "the 'livest' town, for its age and population, that America has ever produced."

"The sidewalks swarmed with people," he wrote, "to such an extent, indeed, that it was generally no easy matter to stem the human tide. The streets themselves were just as crowded with quartz wagons, freight teams and other vehicles. The procession was endless."

During his two years in Virginia City, Twain saw the town grow even busier as undreamed-of wealth poured out of the Comstock silver mines.

"Money was as plenty as dust," he wrote, "every individual considered himself wealthy . . . The 'flush times' were in magnificent flower . . . The great Comstock Lode stretched its opulent length straight through the town from north to south, and every mine on it was in diligent process of development . . . and the blasting, picking and shoveling went on without ceasing, night and day."

Halley's Comet lit up the sky when Samuel Langhorne Clemens was born in Florida, Missouri, on November 30, 1835. Twenty-eight years later he became "Mark Twain" in the pages of the *Territorial Enterprise*. His fellow journalist and roommate, William Wright, was born on May 9, 1829, in Knox County, Ohio. When Clemens arrived in Virginia City, Wright had already become "Dan De Quille."

At Gold Hill in 1859, miners found enough gold to make them feel rich—unaware of the fortune in silver they were throwing away.

The phenomenon of the Comstock—named for an ambitious con man who died broke—began slowly. As early as 1850, members of a Mormon emigrant train enroute to California camped in the Carson Valley and noticed the reddish color of a ravine on the southern side of Mount Davidson. They named the ravine Gold Canyon, then moved on—leaving behind, still hidden, the richest silver deposit ever to be discovered in America.

Later that year, a group of Sonoran Mexicans arrived at Gold Canyon and started digging for gold. Other miners, drifting back from unsuccessful digs in California, joined them. By the middle of 1851, about a hundred prospectors were working their way up the mountain, following a thin stream of placer gold. The miners banded together, loosely, in a makeshift little community called Johntown.

Gold Canyon didn't make them rich. Later geologists estimated the average daily take, between 1851 and 1857, was never more than five dollars. But the stubborn miners kept on digging. Few had any formal training in geology, but they knew gold when they saw it. Most of them didn't recognize the significance of the messy blue mud that got in their way.

A Scientific Approach: The Grosch brothers were exceptions. Educated easterners who had come west during the California Gold Rush of 1849, Ethan and Hosea Grosch arrived in Gold Canyon in 1853. They were disappointed in their hopes for a rich gold strike, but they

Hosea and Ethan Grosch were first to see the value of the "damned blue stuff" other prospectors had discarded. But both died before claiming the silver that made millions for others.

Five years after the Grosch brothers left the Comstock, Dan De Quille wrote to an Idaho newspaper: "Some new strikes have been made in Virginia City, in silver. One is a lead called 'Vermillion lead' and 'Ironside Co.' said to be very good; the price went up from 50 cents to 80 dollars in one day."

knew enough about geology to find encouragement in that blue mud.

For the next two years they wandered in and out of Carson County, Utah Territory—soon to become the separate Territory of Nevada. Early in 1856, the brothers wrote to their father:

"Ever since our return from Utah, we have been trying to get a couple of hundred dollars together for the purpose of making a careful examination of a silver lead in Gold Cañon."

The necessary money turned up and the brothers set to work. Their predictions were confirmed. At the head of the canyon they found two silver veins.

"One of these veins is a perfect monster," they wrote. "We have hopes, almost amounting to a certainty, of veins crossing the Cañon at two other points."

The brothers were right again. They found the two veins of silver—then a third and fourth.

"The rock of the vein looks beautiful," they told their father. ". . . Its colors are violet-blue, indigo-blue, blue-black and greenish-black." When they sent some of the ore for a preliminary assay, the brothers were told it would be worth at least $3,500 a ton.

Keeping their discovery a secret, Ethan and Hosea Grosch staked their claims and went on with their plan. They intended to outline the silver veins as completely as possible, then go back to California to raise enough capital to start serious mining.

In the summer of 1857 their luck ran out. Hosea injured his foot with a pick and died of gangrene. Ethan went on with the plan, but never reached his California bankers.

With Richard Bucke, a Canadian traveling companion, Ethan Grosh set out across the Sierra in November. For more than two weeks, the men were lost in a winter storm. Twelve days after they crawled into a little mining camp called Last Chance, Ethan died.

If Bucke knew about the silver on Mount Davidson, he was too discouraged to follow it up. One of his frozen feet had to be amputated and he went home to Canada to recover. The silver was still a secret.

Enter Mister Comstock: Another Canadian with gold fever found better luck in Gold Canyon and pursued it—even when it was somebody else's luck. Henry Thompkins Paige Comstock drifted into the

Johntown camp in 1856, while the Grosch brothers were quietly exploring veins of silver. When Hosea died and Ethan left for California, Comstock moved into their neat stone cabin and told people he had been promised a share in the Grosch enterprise, in return for keeping claim-jumpers away.

Most historians agree that Comstock had no idea that a fortune in silver lay buried beneath the claims he was protecting. They also doubt that he was ever a Grosch partner. Everybody in town at the time seemed to dismiss Comstock as a lazy braggart who quickly spent all the money he made from tiny traces of gold he managed to find. But the man had an uncanny talent for being in the right place at the right time.

One Johntown inhabitant later remembered Comstock as "an industrious visionary prospector, though little more than half-witted."

The same old-timer recalled another miner who became part of the Comstock legend: "James Finney, 'Old Virginia,' frontier hunter and miner, a man of more than ordinary ability in his class, a buffoon and practical joker, a

A con man who was in the right place at the right time, Henry Comstock gained worldwide fame for discoveries made by others.

"Twain Country," 1861–1868

hard drinker when he could get the liquor, an indifferent worker at anything."

Finney, whose real name may have been Fennimore, had been prospecting in Gold Canyon, without much luck, since 1851. In the winter of 1858–59 he and three companions hit paydirt near the head of Gold Canyon. It was a rich deposit, richer than anything else the miners had found. Finney and his friends immediately staked out four fifty-foot placer claims.

As soon as Comstock heard about Finney's activities, he rounded up some friends and arrived at the same spot to file a fifth claim. The group called the place Gold Hill. Pretty soon the new mine was producing enough gold to pay each man from eight to twenty-five dollars a day. The only problem was that "damned blue stuff."

The Grosch brothers, if they had lived, could have told the Gold Hill miners that they had stumbled upon a treasure far richer than the gold they pounded and washed out of the earth. But the miners, blinded by the glitter of gold dust, simply threw away the blue nuisance.

Soon the entire population of Johntown moved to Gold Hill. A collection of brush huts and tents became the new metropolis of the mountain—for a few months.

Over the ridge, just a mile away from Gold Canyon, other miners were exploring placer gold deposits at the top of Six-Mile Canyon. In June 1859, Patrick McLaughlin and Peter O'Riley made a promising find—specks of gold mixed with blue mud. The two men set out their claims and started washing the gold, still unaware that they had uncovered the top of a great silver lode.

McLaughlin and Riley hardly had time to report their find before Henry T. P. Comstock showed up and accused them of trespassing on his property. It was a ranch, he told them—160 acres of sagebrush and rock—and he owned it all. Even the water they used to wash the gold, he said, came from a spring he'd owned with Finney and another miner.

Comstock blustered on, then appeared to soften. He was a reasonable man, he said, so he'd let them mine his land if they'd share the mining claims with him and a friend. Then he mounted his horse and rode away to find "Old Virginny" Finney.

Nobody really knows what Comstock told Finney, but the legend is that the slick operator bought Finney's share of the spring for a bottle of whiskey and a horse. Now Comstock owned claims at the north and south ends of the lode. With McLaughlin and O'Riley, he formed a company—the Comstock Company—and started mining at Ophir (named for King Solomon's mines). This was the northern end of what he called "the Comstock lode."

This cluster of tents near Gold Hill, Nevada, around 1860, would soon become Virginia City.

The Damned Blue Stuff: He still didn't know it was a silver lode. The "damned blue stuff" was still being thrown away. Some of it was carted down the mountain to Fuller's Crossing in the Truckee Meadows, just to get it out of the way.

The color of the discarded ore intrigued two men in the Meadows who suspected it was more than just mud. B. A. Harrison, a rancher, and J. F. Stone, a trader, collected some of the ore in two sacks and sent it off to California to be analyzed.

Two professional assayers in Grass Valley and Nevada City confirmed the hopes of Harrison and Stone. The ore, they agreed, was tremendously rich in silver. Melville Atwood, the Grass Valley assayer, later said his sample indicated a value of $3,000 per ton in silver and $876 in gold.

Such reports were to be kept confidential, but two insiders heard enough to send them racing over the mountains to the Ophir diggings. James Walsh and Joseph Woodward bought shares in the new mine before the owners had time to realize how rich they were.

When Walsh and Woodward went home to Grass Valley, they spread the word—and the silver rush began. In San Francisco, speculators heard the news and joined the throngs heading east to "Washoe."

In carnival-barker prose, J. Ross Browne wrote a contemporary account of the phenomenon:

> What rumor is this? Whence come these silvery strains wafted to our ears from the passes of the Sierra Nevada? As I live, it is a cry of Silver! Silver in Washoe! Not gold now, you silly men of Gold Bluff; you Kern Riverites; you daring explorers of British Columbia! But SILVER—solid, pure SILVER! Beds of it, ten thousand feet deep! Acres of it, miles of it! Hundreds of millions of dollars poking their backs up out of the earth ready to be pocketed.

News of gold discoveries in what was then Utah Territory brought in a swarm of prospectors eager to join "The Rush to Washoe."

A handful of foresighted San Franciscans moved quickly to pocket their share of those dollars. Offering to buy Gold Hill claims at fifty dollars a foot, they easily persuaded the original claim-holders to part with their valuable shares. To men accustomed to living on five dollars a day, a single check for two or three thousand seemed a fortune.

Even "Old Virginny," who had managed to hold on to his Gold Hill claim, sold it for twenty-five hundred dollars and rushed off to the nearest saloon. It was his love of whiskey that eventually provided his ticket to immortality.

A crude town had sprung up around the Ophir diggings, but nobody had time to give it a formal name. Most miners called it simply, "Ophir." Other names were suggested, but didn't stick—until Old Virginny Finney stumbled out of a saloon one night and tripped, dropping his bottle of whiskey. The bottle broke and spilled its contents on the ground.

Local legend says Finney dipped his hand into the puddle of whiskey and sprinkled it around, saying, "I baptize this place Virginia Town!" So now the place had a name. Eventually upgraded to "Virginia City," the name lasted and the crude mining camp evolved into a sophisticated city, capital of the Comstock.

As for the man whose name had come to mean untold riches, Henry T. P. Comstock outsmarted himself when he sold his claims to James Walsh for $11,000. He stayed around Virginia City for a few years, spending his money and hoping to repeat earlier successes, but his lucky streak was over. He was penniless in 1870 when he died in Bozeman, Montana. Some say he killed himself. Others claimed he was murdered.

When Virginia City was incorporated in February 1861, its post office had been in operation for more than a year. During that time the town had mushroomed. Before Sam Clemens walked into the *Territorial Enterprise* office in 1862, the population of Virginia City had grown to more than 3,000—nearly half the 6,857 people counted by the first census in the Territory of Nevada. It was to double and triple before he left.

The new territory, created March 3, 1861, had been a western chunk of Utah Territory, some 63,000 square miles. A year later, the federal government added another strip of Utah to Nevada. There would be more additions after Nevada became the 36th state of the Union, October 31, 1864: Utah lost more territory to Nevada in 1866 and Arizona gave away a triangular tip of southern desert in 1867.

I nternational Flavors: For twenty years of ups and downs—from prosperity to depression and back—Virginia City was the biggest, busiest city in the raw, new state. It was also the most cosmopolitan, attracting waves of fortune-seekers from around the world.

In *Restless Strangers*, a study of Nevada's immigrants, historian Wilbur Shepperson counts the numbers of foreign-born workers in Virginia City at the height of the mining boom:

"Of the 2,770 men gainfully employed in the mining industry on the Comstock Lode in June, 1880," he wrote, "816 were Irish born, 640 English born, 544 from other foreign nationalities and only 770 American born."

Tracing the social influences of Chinese, Italian, German, Mexican, Welsh, Jewish, French, Irish and English customs on the town, he examines a full year of Virginia City events described in the local newspaper.

"The extent of the foreign activity," he wrote, "was emphasized by a page in the *Territorial Enterprise* of June 8, 1875. Page 3 carried reports of a German gymnastic competition, a German band concert, . . . a review of 'The Flower Girl of Paris' given at the opera house . . . a Welsh language sermon in the Miners' Union Hall, and a gathering to celebrate the adoption of the Italian constitution. Announcements told of the receipt of uniforms for the Irish-American band . . . and a Cornish wrestling match."

The same year's calendar included a Chinese New Year celebration, with parades and fireworks. On the Fourth of July, a French balloonist "dazzled the people of the Comstock with balloon ascensions of the Montgolfier type."

More than a century later, hundreds of balloonists flock to Reno each September for the annual Great Reno Balloon Races. And some of the international flavor of old Virginia City still clings to modern Reno.

French and Spanish Basques arrived at the turn of the century and became an influential part of Nevada's ethnic mix. Basque-American writer Robert Laxalt immortalized them in *Sweet Promised Land*, a tribute to his father: "These were the men of leather and bronze who had been rich as barons one day and broke and working for wages the next, who had ridden big and powerful horses, and who had met in the lonely desert and talked a while, hunkering over a sagebrush fire and a blackened coffeepot, and, even though they had battled with life, they had learned to accept it, because they had learned first to bow their heads to the winter blizzards and the desert sun. And my father was one of them."

Names like Capriotti and Drabczyk are sprinkled through the Reno telephone book along with Gonzalez, Goldstein, Doyle, McCarran, Wakamatsu and Wong. They may be outnumbered by Smiths and Joneses, but they're no less prominent.

Reno's Painful Memories: Over the years, Reno has gone through periods of racial and ethnic prejudice that led to unflattering labels like "Mississippi of the West." Blacks, Italians, Germans, Japanese and Basques have suffered insults and discrimination, from time to time. But the city's most painful memories of prejudice involve a cruel campaign in 1908 to drive out Chinese residents.

Reno's Chinatown, at the turn of the century, occupied valuable property east of Virginia Street and north of the Truckee River. The city wanted it—so they simply destroyed Chinatown, leaving families homeless at the beginning of winter.

It was an official act and it drew protests from Washington to San Francisco. Newspapers across the country published pictures of women carrying babies and old men with crutches being driven from their homes. Displaced citizens signed petitions and demanded damages, but city officials ignored the criticism.

They argued that the destruction had probably saved the community from a major epidemic. Chinatown was "unsanitary," they said. Anyway, it was an eyesore.

"For the Chinese," Shepperson wrote, "the state was never a promised land; rather, it became a land of heartbreak and defeat."

Earlier, in Virginia City at the height of its prosperity, the Chinese were accepted—along with Cornish miners and French charcoal burners—as part of the cosmopolitan picture.

Mark Twain described visits to Virginia City's Chinatown in stories written for the *Territorial Enterprise*. In *Roughing It*, he sums up his view of the Chinese in a slightly superior tone:

"They are a kindly disposed, well-meaning race, and are respected and well treated by the upper classes, all over the Pacific coast. No California *gentleman* or *lady* ever abuses or oppresses a Chinaman, under any circumstances, an explanation that seems to be much needed in the East. Only the scum of the population do it—they and their children; they and, naturally and consistently, the policemen and politicians."

Homeless families gathered around the ashes of Reno's Chinatown after city officials ordered its destruction by fire.
—*Reno Gazette,*
November 11, 1908

Contemporary Views: Visitors to Virginia City, in Mark Twain's day and later, recorded varied impressions of the town. Thomas Starr King, a crusading preacher from San Francisco, went home from a visit in 1863 with an impression of "a city of Ophir holes, gopher holes and loafer holes."

Another San Franciscan wrote, "I have seen more rascality, great and small, in my brief forty days in this wilderness of sagebrush, sharpers and prostitutes than in thirteen years' experience in our not squeamishly moral state of California."

A woman's view of the city, as it was a few years later, was written for the *Overland Monthly*, May 1869, by Louise Palmer, wife of a Virginia City legislator and mining superintendent:

"No man who has ever breathed the air of excitement and speculation of Nevada can live and be content in the quiet of his Eastern birthplace," she wrote. "There is a charm in these rugged mountains which calls him back. . . . There is a saying that one who has been to Nevada can never die until he returns to it.

"We ladies say it is the charm of the cloudless skies that draws us back after our annual visit to 'the bay,' and makes us gladly bear the discomforts or horrors of the journey across the rugged Sierras, to reach our homes over the catacombs beneath the streets of Virginia, or high upon the bleak sides of Mount Davidson."

When Louise Palmer wrote her article, *How We Live in Nevada*, the end of the Civil War was four years in the past and the Union flag flew over the courthouse, along with the blue flag of the five-year-old state of Nevada. In the eight years since incorporation, Virginia City had survived depression as well as periods of wild prosperity.

Transportation was a big problem for the silver mines. Wagonloads of heavy ore had to be hauled down steep, unpaved mountain trails by teams of horses and mules. Everything else—from heavy machinery and water to food, fuel and ladies' bonnets—had to be pulled up the same steep trail.

What Virginia City needed was a railroad link to the rest of the world. William Sharon knew that. As manager of the Virginia City branch of the Bank of California since 1864, Sharon had gained control of mining shares, mills, machinery, water and every other source of profit he could buy. Nicknamed "King of the Comstock," Sharon decreed that a railroad would be built. In 1869 he started construction of the Virginia and Truckee Railroad. It would join the cross-continental Central Pacific at the new depot in Reno.

By this time a number of San Francisco bankers had taken over the mines and were bringing their opulent lifestyle to the Comstock. Some brought their families and settled them into ornate mansions.

After 1876, visitors were put up in style at the new five-story International Hotel where they dined on oysters and venison served on silver plates. They sipped French champagne from delicate crystal and ascended to their rooms on the only hydraulic elevator between Chicago and the coast.

For a festive evening, guests were driven to Piper's Opera House in an ornate coach pulled by horses wearing silver harnesses. In the theater audience, diamond-clad heiresses joined rough miners to watch performers imported from New York and Europe.

The Virginia and Truckee Railroad hauled silver ore down the mountain and brought back luxuries for the new millionaires in Virginia City.

One Hoax Too Many: Mark Twain had left Virginia City long before the Big Bonanza, but he, too, appeared on the stage of Piper's Opera House. His taste for mischief in stories for the *Territorial Enterprise* often got him into trouble, but he was popular with readers. Until he contrived one hoax too many.

In the spring of 1864 he wrote a tongue-in-cheek story about the ladies of Carson City diverting funds from a charity to aid the "Miscegenation Society."

Virginia City—once a metropolis, then almost a ghost town—is now a lively tourist attraction.

In the furor that followed, a reporter for a rival newspaper denounced Mark Twain, who then challenged the reporter to a duel. Warned that he was about to be arrested for demanding this illegal duel, Twain left Virginia City on the next stagecoach to San Francisco.

Next time he saw Virginia City, two years later, he was on a lecture tour, entertaining audiences with tales of his adventures in the Sandwich Islands (Hawaii). Piper's Opera House was jammed for his performance, October 31, 1866. The state of Nevada was exactly two years old.

Mark Twain returned to Virginia City one more time, in April 1868, to lecture at the Opera House. This time he passed through the brand new city of Reno on his way up the mountain. When he returned to his new home in Connecticut, the author said he'd come back to Nevada one day—but he never did.

"Get the facts first, and then you can distort them as much as you like." —Mark Twain

After he left, Virginia City reached the zenith of its prosperity, then declined in the 1880s and '90s until it was almost a ghost town. But Reno, the thriving little town on the Truckee River, was still growing. Money from the Comstock had built the railroad that joined Virginia City and Reno. Now Virginia City was dying and Reno was the most important city in Nevada.

Birth of Sin City

3

Five years before Nevada became a state, a few hundred miners met at Gold Hill to set up a mining district, to provide "protection against the lawless."

On June 11, 1859, the Gold Hill Mining District outlawed murder, assaults, robbery, thefts—and organized gambling. The penalty for anyone who tried to make money by serving as the banker for any game of chance was banishment from the district.

That was the first recorded attempt in the Territory of Nevada to control a habit which has flourished in the area for at least 2,300 years. (Some well-worn bone dice found in southern Nevada were used by the Indians about 300 years before the birth of Christ.)

In 1861 Territorial Governor J. W. Nye asked the first session of the Nevada Territorial Legislature to "pass stringent laws" to control gambling.

"Of all the seductive vices extant," Nye said, "I regard that of gambling as the worst. It holds out allurements hard to be resisted. It captivates and ensnares the young, blunts all moral sensibilities and ends in utter ruin."

The legislators voted to save the 16,000 or so residents of the territory from ruin. Anyone operating a game of chance could be fined $500 or sentenced to two years in prison—or both.

Three years later, when Nevada became a state, reformers and zealots echoed Nye's sentiments.

The first state governor, H. G. Blasdel, saw gambling as an unmitigated evil, and carried on a six-year battle with the state legislature over his proposal to outlaw all games of chance. When the legislature rejected outright prohibition and decided instead to attempt to control gambling, Blasdel vetoed the act. But in 1869 a version of that bill passed (over another Blasdel veto) and

Opposite page
Fight fans swarmed through the Reno streets on July 4, 1910, to see Jack Johnson meet Jim Jeffries in "The Battle of the Century."

with minor changes that law remained in effect for 41 years—from 1869 to 1910.

No Betting on the Ground Floor: One novel feature in the 1869 law was a provision that no game of chance could be played on the ground level of any building, and no sign could be posted on the ground floor telling potential gamblers that they could find a game by going up the stairs.

Those who favored the "second story" provision felt that it would protect the innocent from accidental contamination. If a man walked up to the second floor, he obviously knew what was going on up there, wanted to join in, and was probably beyond redemption.

Backers of the bill argued that the gambling would continue in Nevada whether it was legal or illegal, and that the state and the counties and towns could all benefit from the license fees charged for operating games. In a state that was never very enthusiastic about most taxes, this relatively painless way of collecting some money to support the government was persuasive for many legislators.

While tolerating other such frontier customs as the unlimited sale of liquor and the establishment of clearly identified red-light districts in most Nevada towns, the legislature periodically kept tampering with this basic law governing gambling.

Poker, blackjack, "Chinese lottery," craps, and other games were declared acceptable, while a few in which the player had practically no chance of winning were outlawed. And the impoverished local governments, after being permitted to keep 50 percent of the income from licenses at first, were later awarded 75 percent of this early sin tax.

The most ambitious new law created by the legislators was "An act to prohibit the winning of money from persons who have no right to gamble it away." It was designed to protect anyone who was already in debt and in danger of sinking further into the mire through gambling, and men whose wives and children were dependent on their wages. The bill was passed in 1877, but there seems to be no record of it ever being enforced.

During two dark decades, 1880 to 1900, Nevadans had much more to worry about than gambling. The Comstock mines, the major source of Nevada wealth, after producing more than $38 million in ore in 1876, began to play out, and brought in only $1,400,000 in 1881. One by one the other rich mines

"Gambling, like the state itself, is a creature of questionable birth and ancestry," James W. Hulse wrote in *Forty Years in the Wilderness.* "It has had, since the beginning of Nevada history, the status of a bastard child, since it was pronounced an illegitimate activity in the earliest mining district regulations in the 1850s. It was illegal in Nevada in territorial days and in the first years of statehood. It was legalized in 1869 and disowned again in 1910. . . . It never quite disappeared in the railroad and mining towns, however; at best it went into the back rooms of the saloons."

in the state closed down. Discouraged, the miners and the thousands who depended on them for their income began leaving the state, and the population of Nevada dropped by one-third—sliding from sixty-two thousand (in 1880) to forty-two thousand (in 1900).

During this period of steep decline, there was some talk in Congress of abolishing Nevada's statehood. No state had ever been thrown out of the Union, but some Congressmen were ready to set a precedent.

The Wandering Burro: But in 1900, an impoverished miner named Jim Butler went searching for a missing burro and accidentally stumbled onto the outcroppings of a rich vein of gold and silver at Tonopah, in one of the most remote and desolate areas of southwestern Nevada. This was followed by more than a hundred discoveries in the Tonopah and Goldfield districts, and the two hard decades were over. More than 50,000 people were drawn to the state by the promise of a new bonanza.

Although Reno was far north of the new fields, it benefited from the statewide prosperity, and the town's population jumped from 4,500 in 1900 to 10,867 in 1910.

With the depression behind them, some reformers in Reno decided that the time had come for the town to do something about gambling and other vices.

In 1902, the editor of the *Daily Nevada State Journal* wrote: "Reno is facing a crisis. The citizens of this town have at last awakened to the realiza-

"They came from their homelands for myriad reasons—impending wars, religious persecution, restlessness, lure of adventure, and opportunity. The last reason was the main reason. Trapped by old-world economic caste systems that denied the opportunity to better one's station in life, most came in search of the one key to escape from unchanging station—money."—Robert Laxalt in "The Melting Pot," an essay in *East of Eden, West of Zion*.

After San Francisco refused to serve as host to the Jeffries-Johnson bout, Reno seized the chance to stage it, and greeted 22,000 visitors with this proud banner. Widely condemned, the fight also gained the city national and international attention.

tion that this city is branded throughout the coast as a wide open town, where vice is uncontrolled and crime stalks rampant."

A few years later, the president of the University of Nevada announced that he would not allow students to work or live in downtown Reno, where they might be tempted by prostitutes, bars, and gambling clubs.

In 1908, the Reno Anti-Gambling League and many prominent reformers were convinced that the town was ready to change the local laws. The league called for a special election focusing on an ordinance that would outlaw gambling in the city.

About 1,200 Renoites voted to abolish gambling, but 1,800 opposed the proposed ordinance. But the battle wasn't over. Pressure for statewide action to outlaw gambling was building up, and in 1910 the anti-gambling crusade succeeded.

At a time when many people still worked twelve hours to earn $1, fans paid $30 for an "Inner Circle" seat to the Jeffries-Johnson fight.

Raffish Reno: Reno added to its raffish reputation on July 4, 1910, by staging a prizefight that was publicized around the world. Former champion Jim Jeffries had been persuaded to come out of retirement to meet Jack Johnson, the first black to hold the heavyweight title. The fight was originally scheduled for San Francisco, but reformers there had convinced city officials to cancel the brutal exhibition, and Reno had responded quickly, promising to build a new boxing stadium and to provide everything needed to welcome a huge crowd.

Fans began pouring in long before the match was scheduled to begin.

"Every hotel room in town was taken, and miles of special trains with sleeping cars lined the tracks," Robert Laxalt wrote in his history of Nevada. "Betting activity was feverish. The temper of the crowds was downright dangerous, not only because Jack Johnson was a black, but because he had committed what was then regarded as a scandalous indiscretion. He was living openly at his training camp with a white wife."

On the day of the fight, the *Nevada State Journal* gave major space to the event:

JEFFRIES–JOHNSON BATTLE MAY MARK
THE END OF THE PRIZE FIGHT GAME
and:

NEVER ANOTHER FIGHT LIKE
THE ONE TO BE HELD TODAY

Fighting under a punishing July sun, the aging, over-weight Jim Jeffries (left) had little chance against heavyweight champion Jack Johnson.

The newspaper also expressed its prejudices openly. It wrote of Jeffries, a former world champion who had last fought in 1904: "He will fight for a three-fold purpose: for the praise of his wife, for the exaltation and vindication of the white race and for the glory and honor once won and to be cherished, of the supremacy in the vocation he has adopted."

Whatever his motives for fighting, Jeffries was not well prepared for the long battle under a blazing July sun.

"Jack Johnson battered the aging Jeffries into a helpless pulp, finally putting him out of his misery in the 15th round of a scheduled 45-round fight," Laxalt writes. Jeffries's handlers had thrown in the towel after he was knocked down three times.

The crowd, which had expected a Jeffries victory, was stunned.

"There was a strange silence in the arena after the bout had been stopped that stayed with the spectators for years," Steve Sneddon, sports editor of the *Reno Gazette-Journal*, wrote when looking back at the fight five decades later. "It was a funeral-like silence, some said."

After the bruised and battered Jeffries was helped to his corner, he said to his handlers:

"I couldn't come back, boys. I couldn't come back." And then he added: "Ask Johnson if he will give me his gloves."

While there was no violence in Reno after the fight, there were riots across the country when blacks began celebrating Johnson's victory. Blacks and whites fought in cities from New York to New Orleans, and from Norfolk to St. Louis. At least seven died.

PAST   FUTURE

THE
TURNING POIN

PRESENT

When Will James was serving time in the Nevada State Prison for cattle rustling in 1914, he made this composite sketch illustrating his resolve to turn over a new leaf. Twelve years later he was famous internationally as the author-illustrator of "Smoky the Cowhorse," now a children's classic. His name is inscribed in the Nevada Writers' Hall of Fame in Reno. The original sketch is preserved in the Special Collections Department of the University of Nevada Library.

The spectacle had long-term consequences for Reno. Hundreds of news stories and feature stories were sent out that June and July, and many of them indicated that the little town of 10,867 people had managed to entertain 22,000 fight fans successfully.

The Age of Reform: It was just three months after the Jeffries–Johnson fight that Reno had to adjust to life without legalized gambling. The *San Francisco Examiner*, many of whose readers had grown up thinking you could do almost anything in Reno, treated this turnabout as major news:

NEVADA BANGS DOWN LID ON GAMBLING!

An excited reporter wrote:

"Legalized gambling has drawn its last breath in the United States. . . ."

A Reno casino manager told the reporter that he was about ready to quit anyway. People had an exaggerated idea of how much money could be made from running a gambling club, he said. "As a matter of fact," he said, "there hasn't been enough of it for quite a while to cause us to feel that we are giving up anything."

The *Nevada State Journal* published a rather mournful report on the consequences of the new act:

"Commercial Row is in darkness. Trains are now coming to town virtually empty."

Five years after passing the sweeping anti-gambling bill, the state legislature eased up on some of the restrictions. It was all right to play "social games for drinks and cigars," the legislature declared, "or for prizes of a value of not over two dollars" or to play "Nickel-in-the-slot" machines as long as the payoff was not in cash. Even poker or 21 could be played if "the deal changed after each hand."

But two-dollar bets did not satisfy the real gamblers. They found their way to the new clubs in Reno—half-hidden, dimly lighted, and without identifying signs. There the high-stakes games were usually played late at night, with a tough man with a rasping voice and a two-day beard keeping close watch at the door.

Many of these clubs operated through the 1920s, offering bootleg liquor and barely concealed gambling. The largest, the Bank Club, was owned by two shadowy figures—Bill Graham and Jim McKay.

Graham and McKay had friends who found it convenient to hide out in Reno while the FBI or other law officers were looking for them in Chicago or New York. Among their guests in the late '20s and early '30s were John Dillinger, Baby Face Nelson, and Pretty Boy Floyd—all nationally famous gangsters. These visitors had discovered that the half-hidden gambling clubs were useful for laundering money that federal officials might otherwise be able to trace.

The Great Scam: In the early 1930s Graham and McKay managed to talk some trusting easterners into bringing their bank books and securities to Reno, promising them much higher returns if they would exchange their valuables for other investments.

These exchanges were made through the Riverside Bank in Reno. The victims returned home with worthless pieces of paper, while the securities they had turned over to Graham and McKay were sent by registered mail to New York for quick sale. That turned out to be a mistake by the swindlers: Graham, McKay, and four allies in New York City were indicted in 1934 for using the mails to defraud.

The four New Yorkers who had joined in the million-dollar scam were convicted, largely because of the testimony of Roy Frisch, who had been cashier at the Riverside during the period of the swindles. The trials of Graham and McKay were set for July 1934, in New York, and Frisch was expected to testify. But he didn't make it to court.

In "The Strange Disappearance of Roy Frisch," published in a short-lived Reno magazine, *Reno Pace*, Mark Curtis retraced the last known activities of the missing witness:

"At 240 Court Street on a fairly warm evening in late March (1934), the mother and sisters of Roy Frisch made preparations for a bridge party with friends. Frisch did not care for bridge and was rather restless so his mother suggested that he go to a movie. About 7:45 he donned his gray Fedora hat and said to his sister Alice, 'I'm going to a show and will be home early.'

"Leaving his car in the garage he walked from his home at the corner of Court and Belmont, east to Virginia and thence to the theatre. The cashier at the theatre didn't remember selling Frisch a ticket that evening but the theatre manager said he saw him sitting as usual in the loge section of the balcony.

William J. Graham (left) and James C. McKay were powerful figures in Reno's hidden world of illegal gambling, money laundering, and prostitution until their greed sent them to a federal prison.

"After the show, Frisch walked south on Virginia to Court and turned west for home, passing several friends on the way. A short distance past the sheriff's office, across Sierra Street and on the incline of the little hill, he met another friend with whom he chatted for a few minutes. This was at approximately 10:15 p.m. Somewhere between this point and his home, little more than two blocks away, he walked into oblivion."

For years his mother left the front-porch lights burning all night, hoping for his return.

Others assumed soon after his disappearance that someone—perhaps Baby Face Nelson or Pretty Boy Floyd—had kidnapped him and disposed of him as a favor to Graham and McKay. One convict insisted that Frisch was taken on a 150-mile ride, then shot, and his body dropped down an abandoned mine.

Whatever the explanation, Curtis noted:

"No trace of Roy J. Frisch has ever been found."

The Two-Party Boss: During their period of dominance of Reno affairs, Graham and McKay were widely believed to be silent partners of George Wingfield, a former cowboy and gambler who became the most powerful banker in the state. Wingfield, probably the richest man in Nevada during the 1920s, managed to guide both the Republican and Democratic parties in Nevada from his office in the Reno National Bank. He also owned the Riverside, then the most luxurious Reno hotel and casino, and many believed that he managed to do a little bootlegging on the side.

Along with the Bank Club and some smaller establishments, Graham and McKay owned another enterprise in Reno that became a major tourist attraction. This was the Stockade—perhaps the most famous legal brothel in the United States.

When a stranger crossed the Truckee in search of the Stockade, he would find no signs to guide him. But if he asked a Renoite for directions, the answer he would receive would be a casual, "You looking for the Bull Pen? It's across that little bridge there."

The rickety structure carried this warning:

Bridge Not Safe

After taking the risk and crossing, the stranger would find these words posted on a rough wooden door:

ENTRANCE
No Minors Allowed
No Lady Visitors
No Pictures Taken
Order—Police Dept.

Below that he would see a more ominous note:

DANGER NOTICE TO PUBLIC
These premises have been
abated as being dangerous to
to the public health in that
they have been used to spread
the dangerous communicable
diseases, Syphilis and Gonorrhea.

Prostitution was nothing new in Reno, but it was not quite so open until Bill Graham and Jim McKay set up the Stockade. In *Tough Little Town on the Truckee,* historian John M. Townley comments: "Victorian Reno preferred to ignore its presence, while tacitly enjoying the benefits. . . . No one seriously advocated cleaning up the downtown; the Tenderloin met the demands of visiting ranchers, miners and commercial travelers—to say nothing of Reno itself."

Inside visitors would see 48 cubicles, modeled on a cheap 1920s motel. Each cubicle was occupied by a prostitute who paid $2.50 for eight hours' rent each day. On busy weekends the cribs would operate around the clock.

One curious visitor in the 1930s was a San Francisco writer named Max Miller. He speculated over what newcomers from Kansas or Iowa might feel as they approached the Stockade:

"They are about to observe what they always have longed to observe: flesh glistening and raw, spiced and diademed. They are about to visit the Lost Isle of the Sirens—and not to be arrested for it. . . ."

But then, they were confronted by the business-like interior of the Stockade. It had "all the lushy lust of a hardware store," Miller writes, and was conducted in much the same manner.

"The girls are not allowed to leave the doorways of their compartments to greet visitors. The cribs are of hard red brick, exceptionally hard, each built exactly alike and each containing a stove and a curtained-off workroom behind the diminutive reception room. The doorways have the sameness of post office boxes . . . and the women the sameness of keys in those boxes."

"As for any robust exposure of themselves," Miller wrote, "they would appear overdressed if on a bathing beach on a Sunday. Some wear brief dresses of a ballet-dancer, some wear shorts, some wear slacks, some wear evening gowns. But the visitors, if really interested in a scientific study of contours, would do better by remaining back home in Santa Monica."

Reno's colorful mayor, E. E. Roberts, often made national headlines during the 1920s. His political platform was simple: "I've been trying to make Reno a place where everybody can do what they please, just as long as they don't interfere with other people's rights."

Within the Stockade, "merriment remains a stranger," Miller wrote. "At night sometimes there is music, but this is at the far end, in a building by itself, the beer-hall. A tiny, bored orchestra is there sometimes if visitors can afford to feed the kitty."

It was not an entertaining life for the women, Miller wrote. During his visits, he often saw them standing in the doorways yawning with boredom.

When they left the cribs at the end of their shifts, the women received a stern warning not to "solicit or do business."

"The law of Reno is amazingly blunt and watchful about this," Miller wrote. "A girl has to be caught only once trying it, and out she goes, right out of the Stockade and right out of town. That is why Reno claims to have no street walkers, and the claim certainly seems authentic."

Closer to the center of town, he observed, there was a much handsomer establishment—"The Cottage." It was an "authorized sporting-house for the more exclusive trade."

"So frank is Reno," Miller wrote, "that the owners of 'The Cottage'—a young married couple—are accepted around town with the openness of any other business people. They share in the town's activities, and I saw them, on the husband's birthday, being toasted in the ritziest of Reno bars."

While Reno had adjusted to the change in the anti-gambling laws by moving the clubs underground, many people in the city remembered the years before 1910 fondly, and the hunger for a return to the good old days grew during the 1920s.

The Crusading Candidate: A leader in the campaign to ease up on controls over gambling, divorce, or alcohol was Mayor E. E. Roberts, who launched a lively campaign for reelection in 1931.

Roberts left no one in doubt about where he stood:

"You cannot legislate morals into people, any more than you can legislate love into the hearts of some professed Christians. You can't stop gambling, so let's put it out in the open. Divorce is the only solution when marriages are unhappy. And if I had my way in this Prohibition year, I as mayor of Reno would place a barrel of whiskey on every corner, with a dipper, and a sign saying: 'Help yourself, but don't be a hog'."

On that platform Roberts was overwhelmingly reelected, and the roaring thirties were about to begin. A conservative small-town rancher named Phil Tobin (who had no interest in gambling himself) paved the way for the great change in Reno. He saw that the attempts to outlaw gambling had failed and thought the state and the towns might as well collect some license fees from dice games, card games, and the slot machines. He offered a bill to legalize gambling, and Governor Fred Balzar signed it on March 19, 1931.

Down with Nevada! The national reaction was more frenzied than the advocates had anticipated. *The Los Angeles Times* called Nevada "a vicious Babylon" while the *Kansas City Star* pronounced Reno a combination of "Sodom, Gomorrah and Hell."

The *Chicago Tribune* offered a simple solution to the national disgrace:

CANCEL NEVADA'S STATEHOOD!

Not everyone was horrified. Will Rogers commented that "Nevadans have shaken off the cloak of hypocrisy," and suggested that Wall Street should also license its gamblers.

Undisturbed by the furor, Mayor Roberts observed quietly:

"Now we can do lawfully what Nevada has always done under cover."

But the expected rewards of sin did not appear immediately. The operators of the Reno speakeasies were not very successful in attracting newcomers to their grimy gambling dens. Two outsiders would have to teach them the way to do that—and it would be a while before those strangers would appear to transform the city.

It turned out also that Reno would have to get along without those two prominent citizens, Bill Graham and Jim McKay. Despite the mysterious disappearance of the chief witness against them, they were finally sent off to the pokey in 1937 on charges of using the mail to defraud.

Although some changes were slower in coming than many observers anticipated, Reno managed to get through the depression of the early 1930s because the town had already discovered how to bring in some other important guests: men and women who wanted to shed their mates without complications, explanations—or a long wait.

When the Great Depression struck the state, some uneasy Nevadans remembered the famous "Mormon curse." Mormon pioneer Orson Hyde, who felt he had been cheated because he was never paid for a sawmill he was forced to abandon when he left the state, swore revenge. "You shall be visited by the Lord of hosts with thunder and with earthquakes and with floods," he warned the Nevadans he left behind. "You shall be visited with pestilence and famine until your names are not known among men for you have rejected the authority of God, trampled upon His laws and His ordinances. You have given yourself up to debauchery, abominations, drunkenness and corruption. If there is an honest man among you, I would advise him to leave, but let him not go to California for safety for he will not find it there."

Matrimonial Games

4

"I'm going to Reno!" the angry wife announced in countless movies of the 1930s. Audiences knew exactly what she meant. By that time, Reno was the divorce capital of the world.

Who hadn't heard about those "quickie" Nevada divorces that made headlines back east? If a Broadway celebrity wanted freedom from a spouse, New York divorce courts required proof of adultery. No other reason would do—and the process was slow.

In Reno it was so much easier. Just visit the town for six weeks and become a legal resident of Nevada. After that, the restless one could join a line of divorce-seekers at the Washoe County Court House, spend no more than ten minutes answering the judge's questions and—presto! Divorce granted—on grounds no more specific than "incompatibility" or "mental cruelty."

In a scene from *The Women*, Clare Boothe's 1936 Broadway play, four friends from New York are in Reno to break out of troubled marriages.

When the much-married Countess deLage proposes a celebration of a friend's divorce, young Peggy Day protests:

PEGGY:	*Oh, Countess deLage, I don't think a divorce is anything to celebrate.*
COUNTESS:	*Wait 'til you've lost as many husbands as I have, Peggy . . . Married, divorced, married, divorced! But where Love leads I always follow. So here I am in Reno.*

As soon as her divorce becomes final, the countess intends to marry a

Opposite page
When wealthy celebrities came to Reno for quick divorces in the 1930s, they found gambling clubs clustered on Virginia Street.

cowboy—with whom, she says, "I've been galloping madly over the desert all day!" The countess is about to become a statistic—one of the many divorcées who came to Reno to shed one mate and find another.

The playwright's vision of Reno, designed for laughs, exaggerates and simplifies Nevada's divorce mill of the thirties, but Clare Boothe knew the scene firsthand. She had spent three months in Reno in 1929—before the residence requirement was reduced to six weeks—waiting for her divorce from New York millionaire George Brokaw. During that time, five years before her marriage to *Time-Life* publisher Henry Luce, Boothe met dozens of women whose stories provided later inspiration for some of her characters in *The Women.*

She met many of these divorcées at the home of Washoe District Judge George A. Bartlett and his wife. During his twenty years on the bench, Judge Bartlett granted thousands of divorces. It was Bartlett who introduced into the Nevada divorce statute a clause that made it unnecessary for a divorce-seeker to make specific charges against a mate.

"In this way," he said, "the present morbid practice of publicizing the intimate details of divorce action will be avoided."

One Hollywood starlet, grateful for her freedom, said she owed it all to "Judgie." Others picked up the nickname—and it stuck. Everybody in Reno knew "Judgie" Bartlett.

The Bartletts loved giving parties where authors and movie stars exchanged chit-chat with opera singers, prizefighters and medical researchers. Cornelius Vanderbilt, Tallulah Bankhead, Sherwood Anderson, Katherine Ann Porter, Jack Dempsey and Paul de Kruif were just a few of the famous names on their guest lists.

Those were the days when local newspapers kept track of divorces and marriages and presented the numbers like baseball scores.

A headline in the *Nevada State Journal*, December 31, 1931:

DIVORCE DECREES OF 1931
NEARLY DOUBLE THOSE OF 1930
4248 Get Marital Freedom;
Marriage Licenses
Larger Than Divorce Actions

Nevada's easy divorce laws had shocked sedate easterners since territorial days. Miners who came to find fortunes in the Comstock often found new lives and new loves. If they were going to establish new families—legally—they had to be sure of legal separation from former mates.

As early as 1871, Nevada courts declared that anyone who had been a resident of the state for six months could obtain a divorce without documenting charges of adultery. By 1899, Nevada's reputation for easy divorce-with-few-questions-asked had spread around the world.

Across the Atlantic Ocean, a British lord and his wife were convinced their nine-year marriage had been a mistake. Just a year after Lord John Russell married Mabel Scott in 1890, his bride had tried to divorce him—unsuccessfully. British law and the Anglican Church frowned on divorce, but that didn't keep Lord Russell from looking around for a new ladyfriend.

When Mollie Cooke Somerville became his constant companion, he wanted to marry her—but she had already divorced a previous husband and was still married to another. The Church didn't approve at all.

Lord Russell's Shocking Divorce: So, in 1899, Lord Russell and Mollie came to Nevada. They settled at Lake Tahoe and waited the required six months. As soon as they became legal Nevada residents, each was granted a quiet divorce from an absent spouse. A few days later, April 5, 1900, they came to Reno and were married by District Judge Ben Curler.

No problem—until the Russells returned to England and set up housekeeping. When the first Lady Russell filed a divorce action in London—on grounds of bigamy—the newspapers noticed. The House of Lords summoned Judge Curler from Nevada to give testimony and Lord Russell was arrested.

Judge Curler backed up Lord Russell's claim that he considered the Nevada divorce legal, but the House of Lords found Russell guilty of bigamy. He was sentenced to three months in Holloway Prison. After his release, he and Mollie were married again.

Nevada District Judge Ben Curler was called to London in 1901 to testify for Lord John Russell in the bigamy case against him.

At the time, Lord Russell told reporters he was going back to Nevada to become a rancher, but he changed his mind. Eventually, he divorced Mollie, too, and married an Australian writer.

When Russell died in 1931, his brother—the philosopher Bertrand Russell—succeeded him in the House of Lords. Twenty years later, the third Lord Russell came to Reno to get a divorce. By that time, Reno divorces had become commonplace.

Half a century earlier, the older Russell's divorce had caused a scandal in

Victorian London—and had established Reno's reputation among wealthy socialites on both sides of the Atlantic.

In Pittsburgh, in the spring of 1905, the president of United States Steel told his wife he was leaving for Europe with a young California actress. A few months later, the wife headed for Reno.

William Ellis Corey and Laura Corey had been married since 1883 and had one child, but the steel tycoon had a wandering eye. When it wandered so far that Corey was seen more often with the actress than his wife, Laura Corey decided she'd had enough.

A cartoonist of the early 1930s offered a daring suggestion: Divorce may be "The Cure."

Her arrival in Reno, her establishment of residence and her eventual divorce were big news back East. Headlines hinted at scandalous details and newspaper circulation figures soared. Readers couldn't wait to see the latest installment.

A Reno lawyer, seeing his chance to cash in on the town's notoriety, started advertising his services in New York newspapers. Asking himself where he might find the highest concentration of potential clients, William Schnitzer also advertised in Broadway theater programs, publicizing the advantages of a Reno divorce. His ads attracted the attention of discontented spouses who soon headed for Reno.

As their numbers increased, the town recognized a new source of prosperity to rival the Comstock mining boom. By 1910, the Nevada divorce business was celebrated in popular songs of the day. Trendy young couples cranked up their Victrolas and danced to the sound of Billy Murray singing:

> *I'm on my way to Reno,*
> *I'm leaving town today*
> *Give my regards to all the boys*
> *And girls along Broadway*
> *Once I get my liberty,*
> *No more wedding bells for me*
> *Shouting the battle cry of Freedom!*

Reno became a synonym for divorce. As more and more wealthy celebrities arrived in Reno to cancel their marriage vows, the city was denounced from pulpits across the country. All over Nevada, moral reformers campaigned to clean up the state's image. By 1913, these reformers had persuaded the state legislature to expand the mandatory residence requirement from six months to a year.

Sure enough, the flood of divorce-seekers diminished. So did the ring of cash registers. In 1914 a Reno attorney estimated that the city's lawyers and businesses were losing at least a million dollars a year because of the slowdown in the divorce trade. He and his colleagues urged the 1915 legislature to change the residence requirement back to six months. The lawmakers complied.

Within a few months, Reno was back to normal. Once again, trains from the east were delivering expensively dressed visitors ready to become Nevadans for six months. Reporters haunted the railroad station, hoping every day to recognize a celebrity whose name would ensure headlines.

Discontent in Hollywood: In 1920, the really big name was Mary Pickford, "America's Sweetheart." The silent screen star had decided to leave her first husband, Owen Moore, to marry Douglas Fairbanks, the dashing actor. Attempting to avoid publicity, the actress used her legal name, Gladys Moore, when she arrived at a ranch near Minden, south of Reno.

Two weeks later, Owen Moore showed up in Minden and was handed divorce papers. When the case came up before District Judge Frank P. Langan, he granted the divorce, ignoring the six-months residence requirement.

Was the divorce legal—or wasn't it? Newspapers speculated. Unquestionably, the actress was not a permanent resident of Nevada. As soon as Judge Langan handed down his decree, she returned to California to marry Fairbanks.

Gossips predicted trouble. They said the sheriff of Douglas County had been bribed to serve the divorce papers and that Judge Langan had been paid $1,000 to call a special session of his court to hear the case. Nobody proved the rumors, but newspapers managed to keep the Pickford divorce story alive for the next two years.

"Reno," one reporter wrote, had become "the most interesting city between Chicago and San Francisco." And it wasn't long before Washoe County struck a new bonanza.

In 1927, Reno weddings became almost as popular as Reno divorces. That was the year the California legislature passed what was known as the "anti-gin" marriage law, making it necessary for California couples to wait three days between marriage license and wedding ceremony. So the impatient ones simply drove across the mountains to Reno—where there was no waiting period.

Even in Reno, matrimonial knots were still more easily tied than untied.

"America's Sweetheart," Mary Pickford, was granted a controversial Nevada divorce in 1920.

The six-months Nevada residence requirement for divorces was cut in half by the 1927 legislature, but it still took three months to become a Nevadan. Nevertheless, three months was a far shorter wait than other states required.

"Reno was a hot number in those days," newspaper publisher John Sanford recalled in his oral history. "After that was when the so-called divorce mill really began to grind. . . . The reporters who covered the courthouse and the correspondents for outside papers and the wire services all kept copies of the Social Register on hand. And as fast as these cases'd be filed, every morning, they'd go thumbing through there to see who it was."

Among the correspondents waiting on the courthouse steps was Max Stern of the *Pittsburgh Press.* One of his stories, published November 25, 1928, reported:

"Two thousand matrimonial invalids now crowd the Sagebrush Metropolis waiting for the new quick divorces, spending over $5,000,000 a year and bringing the state of Nevada the biggest boom it has known since Gold Rush Days."

Another young reporter who came to Reno in 1928 was William B. Berry, an ambitious freelancer who took a job as a linotype operator at the *Nevada State Journal.* He sold divorce stories to United Press, pictures to the Associated Press and celebrity interviews to newspapers across the country.

Bill Berry Remembers: In 1931, when Nevada divorce laws reduced the required three-months residence period to six weeks, Berry's freelance opportunities multiplied. His by-line turned up everywhere.

"My stories made the front pages—with headlines THAT big," Berry recalled more than 60 years later. His biggest break came in 1941 when he told the world that Gloria Vanderbilt was getting a Reno divorce from Pat DeCicco to marry white-haired conductor Leopold Stokowski.

The millionairess recalled her meetings with the reporter in *Black Knight—White Knight,* her 1987 memoir based on her own diaries:

"Bill Berry is a constant companion, following me everywhere, friendly as pie, questioning me as if he knows nothing, so I'll be drawn into explaining things and talking a lot. L. is already on the train and I'm desperate as there's no way to warn him."

Stokowski hated personal publicity, she explained, and she was determined to protect him from reporters. "He has stressed to me that if ever questioned by reporters I'm to keep repeating, no matter what, 'I never answer personal questions I never answer personal questions I never answer personal questions I never answer personal questions. . . .'"

So Gloria left her rented car parked outside the Hotel Riverside, hoping to divert Berry, and drove off in another car with a woman companion, in the middle of the night, to meet Stokowski at the railroad station in Truckee.

When Stokowski stepped down from the train, "wearing the hat he always wears for disguise," guess who appeared on the platform to welcome him? Bill Berry grabbed the famous conductor's hand and said, "Welcome to Truckee, the back door to Nevada!"

The Hotel Riverside became a temporary home for rich, famous, and notorious divorce-seekers.

"He thought Bill Berry was a railroad employee," Vanderbilt wrote—until the reporter announced, "I represent the New York *Daily News*." Stokowski choked, while Berry—asking questions all the way—followed him to the car where Gloria was waiting. As they drove away through the snow, Berry wished the couple "all the happiness in the world." At that moment, the bride-to-be recalled, she was so happy she loved everybody—"Bill Berry, too, yes I did!"

The Vanderbilt story brought Berry a generous offer from the New York *Daily News*. After that, he became the paper's full-time Reno correspondent—until 1964.

When Berry first arrived in Reno, most wealthy divorce-seekers rented houses for the required three months or lived at the Hotel Riverside. A few of them found more privacy on ranches outside of town.

R anches for Dudes: Cattle rancher Neil West, recognizing an opportunity when he saw one, built cabins on his property west of Pyramid Lake and rented them to "dudes" who wanted a taste of home on the range. By 1931, when the six-weeks divorce law went into effect, other horse and cattle ranches—most of them near Pyramid Lake—were offering accommodations to visitors.

In *Nevada Towns and Tales*, Nancy J. Jackson describes the most popular divorce ranches of the time:

"There were about 4,800 divorce-seekers in Nevada in 1931 when a peculiarly Nevada kind of dude ranch began to appear, built for the trade. They were usually full before the paint was dry on the new kitchen.

". . . All of these were alike in many ways, distinguished by the personalities of the managers and changing as the management changed. Some were, like the Flying ME, large houses with dining rooms and living rooms shared by all the guests; some, like Washoe Pines and Pyramid Lake ranches, had cabins for guests behind and around a main building that was office, kitchen, dining and living room. All had horses, a wrangler, and sometimes a host-cum-wrangler as well, a cook, maids and all the necessary garages, barns, paddocks, fences and nearby trails."

Journalist Lloyd Boles, a high school student when Reno was the country's divorce capital, remembers his own after-school job at Lawton Hot Springs, a favorite refuge for eastern divorce-seekers.

"I used to drive a 1935 Dodge station wagon down to the Reno railroad station to pick up guests," he recalled. "Mark Yori, the owner of the resort, would point out socialites when they registered—but I was just a kid, so it didn't mean an awful lot to me."

What DID mean a lot to a teen-age boy was meeting a famous movie star. Boles was working in the produce department of a Reno supermarket one day when he was suddenly aware of an exotic perfume and noticed a set of bright green fingernails hovering over the lettuce. He looked up—into the luminous eyes of Paulette Goddard.

"She was here to get a divorce from Charlie Chaplin," Boles explained. "She was staying in a bungalow near the market and she asked me to carry her groceries home." Half a century later, Boles still has the silver dollar the actress gave him for a tip.

In *The American Mercury*, a literary magazine of the period, "Reno the Naughty" was the title of a slightly patronizing article by Anthony Turano, who described the town as he saw it in the mid-thirties. The divorce business, he said, was bringing in something like two million dollars a year.

"Thanks to this artificial payroll," Turano wrote, "Reno was scarcely aware of the Depression until 1931 when the total collapse of the Wingfield fortunes caused three of the four Reno banks to close their doors. And even then, the recovery was very speedy, largely because the wise men and women of the East continued to arrive, bearing gifts."

Turano went on at some length about the divorce-seekers ("seventy-five percent of whom are women") and their need to escape boredom "during their ordeal of solitude among strangers."

Dude ranches, the author said, offered all the comforts expected by a jaded divorcée. "In addition to private bath and dainty food, she has daily access to steed and saddle, together with the services of a vaquero in full regalia."

Turano was skeptical about the authenticity of these buckaroos. "Of

In *The City of Trembling Leaves* Walter Van Tilburg Clark called Reno "the ersatz jungle, where the human animals, uneasy in the light, dart from cave to cave under steel and neon branches, where the voice of the croupier halloos in the secret glades, and high and far, like light among the top leaves, gleam the names of lawyers and hairdressers on upstairs windows. . . ."

A Short History of Reno

course," he commented, " such cowboys are usually synthetic: their chaps and bandanas are more redolent of cheap perfume than the realistic scent of the corral. Very few of them know the difference between a saddle horn and an automobile siren, but they are all competent gigolos, respectful listeners, and reliable consolers of unhappy bitter-halves."

Some divorcées—like the fictional Countess deLage of *The Women*—married cowboys. Others married their lawyers. A good many married somebody they met in Reno and settled down for good. Even the haughty Turano had to admit that these marriages usually lasted.

"Permanent residents," he wrote, "generally regard divorce as a specialized activity that should be respected for revenue only."

The Wedding Bonanza: Weddings became big business for Reno during World War II. More than eighteen thousand couples were married in Washoe County in 1945 alone. Judges performed more than half of these ceremonies and district judges began an informal competition—a "wedding derby" to see who could perform the most marriages.

Judge A. J. Maestretti was the 1946 champion with a score of 5,306 weddings, compared to 5,046 performed by Judge William McKnight. The following year, McKnight moved ahead with 5,888 weddings. Maestretti's score was 5,714. Thirteen other judges accounted for 18,445 marriages and 78 clergymen shared the other 8,104.

All these statistics were reported conscientiously by the *Reno Evening Gazette*. During July 1950, when 2,489 Reno weddings were counted in a single month, the newspaper explained, "County officials attribute the increased business and the youth of the couples to the Korean War." Ages of most altar-bound couples that month ranged from 18 to 25.

Reno weddings outnumbered divorces in 1952 when this headline in the *Gazette* reminded readers that marriage and divorce were a multi-million-dollar business:

Washoe County Celebrates Twenty-fifth Anniversary Of Marriage-Divorce Mill

"Just how long the bonanza will continue is anybody's guess," wrote the unnamed reporter. "The Nevada legislature isn't expected to alter the divorce laws in the near future, but lawmakers in the neighboring state of California could throw a monkey wrench into the wheels of the marriage business at any time."

It didn't happen. California had repealed its "anti-gin marriage law" of 1927—requiring a three-day wait between the issuance of a marriage license and the performance of the ceremony—but the state now required a premarital medical examination. That took time. Impatient couples still flocked to Nevada for weddings.

Reno didn't get all the business. In the early 1950s, Las Vegas was becoming a formidable rival. Two hotels in the southern city, El Rancho Vegas and the Last Frontier, tried to capture a share of Reno's divorce bonanza, advertising "fun in the sun" for those awaiting residency papers.

"The hotels didn't do a lot of business," Jefferson Graham reported in *Vegas: Live and in Person*. "Reno was for divorces. Vegas was for weddings—especially those involving Hollywood stars, such as Mickey Rooney and Elaine Mahnken (1952), Joan Crawford and A. N. Steele (1955) . . . Paul Newman and Joanne Woodward (1958). . . ." Graham's list recalls the wedding of Elvis and Priscilla Presley in 1967—and more celebrity marriages in the 1980s.

Celebrities set the pattern and others followed. California secretaries, store managers, truck drivers and runaway teens headed for Vegas to tie the knot. Just a day's drive or a two-hour flight from Los Angeles, Las Vegas offered economical wedding ceremonies—complete with minister, flowers, candlelight, music and "optional extras"—in lavishly-decorated wedding chapels.

These were commercial enterprises. Critics compared them to fast-food restaurants—"the McDonald's of matrimony"—but their services were far less troublesome, time-consuming and expensive than the average traditional church wedding. And far more festive than a ten-minute civil ceremony in a courthouse. So the wedding business boomed in Las Vegas.

Reno didn't intend to be left behind. The number of divorces had declined in the 1950s, when Mexico became a favored divorce spot for the rich and famous, but hundreds of couples were still lining up for marriage licenses at the Washoe County Courthouse. In a matter of minutes—once the license was issued—they could be married by a judge. No fuss and bother.

If brides and bridegrooms wanted more traditional trimmings, without the planning and expense of full-scale church weddings, some of them traveled to Las Vegas—until Venila and Joe Melcher opened Reno's first commercial wedding chapel in 1956.

Strategically located next door to the Washoe County Courthouse, the

Melchers' chapel made it easy for a bridal couple to exchange vows a few minutes after picking up the license. No waiting. A local minister was called in to perform the ceremony, and everything was official.

Soon, to accommodate a brisk demand, the Melchers moved their operation across the street to a small white house facing a tiny, triangular green park. It became the Park Wedding Chapel, permanently decorated with flowers and candles, always ready on short notice to provide a church-like setting for an informal wedding or a full-dress ceremony.

The word got around fast. Couples from San Francisco to Seattle appeared at the chapel and waited for turns at the altar. Seeing a chance to cash in on the wedding rush, other entrepreneurs opened wedding chapels in downtown Reno—near the courthouse, near the bus station, near casinos.

When guests arrived at the Hotel Riverside in the 1970s, the first thing they saw was a ground floor wedding chapel, promising to take care of all details—flowers, music, photographs, souvenirs and limousine service. When the MGM Grand Hotel and Casino opened in 1978, a lavish wedding chapel was installed in the shopping arcade, next to a flower shop and a photographer's studio. When Bally's took over the MGM Grand, and after Bally's became the Reno Hilton, the chapel remained.

Across from the courthouse, the Park Wedding Chapel is always ready for a ceremony—with music and flowers.

Hasty Weddings: Some "chapels" were makeshift storefront operations advertising bargain rates. When unsuspecting couples came in for the fifteen-dollar wedding, they might discover a list of unavoidable "extras" and a sign on the wall warning, "No Refunds." Some proprietors included a book of casino coupons in the price of the wedding.

These casual enterprises, usually displaying banks of artificial flowers in the window, catered to impulsive couples who walked in on the spur of the moment. If a bride wearing jeans wanted to rent a dress for the occasion, the manager would lead her to a rack of finery-for-hire. Wedding rings? Right there in the display case.

"These are temporary rings," a saleswoman explained. "They're genuine fourteen-carat gold electroplate, made to last three months—or maybe a year. You can't expect a permanent ring for ten dollars."

Some storefront chapels opened and closed without fanfare. A few were left in 1985 when Lincoln Curtis, a young Reno filmmaker, introduced "True Love," a 45-minute documentary shown on public television. Without commentary, the film recorded scenes in a variety of wedding establishments in

Reno and Tahoe.

One segment of "True Love" explores the reasons couples give for choosing to be married in a commercial wedding chapel:

"It's convenient."

"Less expensive than a church wedding."

"More solemn than a justice of the peace."

"We don't believe in churches."

"Didn't want anything fancy for a second marriage."

One thoughtful young bride explains, "If we got married at home, our parents would be involved. They'd invite hundreds of people and spend thousands of dollars. We didn't want all that fuss, so we came to Reno to avoid the hassle."

In the 1990s, Reno's wedding chapels continue to attract couples from California and beyond—including visitors from Europe and the Pacific. Brochures for "Unique Reno Weddings" are displayed at the downtown Visitors Bureau and in the courthouse lobby. Anyone who picks up a marriage license at the courthouse can walk out the door and find three chapels within a few steps: the Starlite and Heart of Reno Chapels on Court Street and the Park Chapel across Virginia Street.

Challenging the competition, the Starlite advertised discount rates in the summer of 1991. Twenty-two dollars, said the ad, included wedding service, music, witness, cassette recording of the ceremony, a marriage scroll—and free parking.

"Present this card before ceremony . . . Minister's gratuity optional."

Next door, the Heart of Reno Chapel offered three different settings in a choice of colors, each accommodating up to fifty guests, and private rooms for receptions. Prices ranged from thirty-five dollars for a basic civil marriage to three hundred dollars for a formal service with all the trimmings, including a videotape of the ceremony.

Around the corner at the Park Wedding Chapel (identified in its brochures as "Reno's Oldest Wedding Chapel") a hostess explained prices to a prospective bride:

"For thirty dollars," she said, "you can have a service in the small chapel with no more than ten guests. Or you can have twenty people in the larger chapel for sixty dollars. That includes background music. To invite more than twenty guests—but no more than forty—you'd pay eighty dollars."

Park Chapel manager Joe Melcher, grandson of the original Joe, rejected the notion that commercial weddings are somehow less serious than church

When Reno columnist Rollan Melton interviewed "Marrying Judge" Ted Lunsford about the 50,000 weddings he had performed since 1958, the judge revealed some insights: "Men were by far the more nervous. Some couples had to be virtually propped up at the altar. A few came close to fainting. . . . A number of couples came in, left their marriage licenses with him and never came back. One couple came to him a total of four times in a single day, backed out each time and never did marry."

ceremonies.

"Most of the couples who come in here have minimal plans," he said. "They just walk in. But this is not a clown show. We try to maintain a certain level of decorum. Although we're a commercial operation, our ministers expect people to behave the way they would in a church."

Young Melcher reported a decline in the wedding business in recent years. "Saturdays aren't what they used to be," he said in 1991. "We used to do sixty or seventy weddings on a typical summer Saturday. Now we're lucky if we do thirty-five."

Reno divorces have declined, too. As early as 1970, most of the old dude ranches had disappeared. As other states gradually adopted more lenient divorce laws, fewer disillusioned spouses found it necessary to come to Reno. Still, the city's reputation persisted into the 1990s.

"There's a lot of misinformation out there about how easy it is to get a divorce in Reno," said attorney Jerold M. Young, a specialist in family law. "People write to us from everywhere—especially from New York and Florida. Some of them think it's possible to get a divorce here in twenty-four hours."

Not so, Young explains, "It's still necessary to live in Nevada at least six weeks—with *intent to remain*—if you want a Nevada divorce. Some judges can be very insistent about that 'intent to remain.' Still, we hear from people who expect overnight decisions. If we ask where that information came from, they say, 'Oh, everybody knows how easy it is in Reno!'"

A Reno tradition: glittering casino musicals evolved from the traveling tent shows that once brought banjo music and jokes to isolated miners.

Millionaires and Movie Stars 5

Reno was not severely affected by the 1929 depression at first, but by late 1931 everything slowed down, including the flow of gamblers from California.

During this period, a man named Norman Biltz worked with several other Nevadans on a plan to populate the state with about seventy-five millionaires who had managed to survive the crash.

Biltz, who was later given the title "The Duke of Nevada" by *Fortune* magazine, went to Carson City to test the idea on Governor Fred Balzar. Biltz and his collaborators assured the governor that they could bring many of the wealthiest men in the United States to Nevada if they could promise them that by coming here they could escape the state income taxes, sales taxes, gift taxes, and inheritance taxes they faced in California and other states.

After Biltz described the sales pitch they planned to use on the wealthiest people in the country, Balzar gave him a letter "pretty much to the effect that he was sure we would state the advantageous tax laws of Nevada honestly, but if we made a mistake, he would attempt to make [the state's tax laws] fit our mistake."

With this open-ended endorsement from the governor, Biltz began searching for millionaires who would be attracted by the idea of a tax-free future in Nevada. He discovered that someone had compiled a list of people who were worth $20 million or more, even during the depressed 1930s, and with his collaborators he put out a special magazine for them: *Nevada: The Last Frontier.*

"In mailing them," he remembered, "we would have a leather binder made with their name on them, so it wouldn't end up in the waste-paper basket."

Biltz and the others were not doing this entirely as a public service. Biltz owned thousands of acres near Lake Tahoe, and was a partner to other major landowners.

The First Millionaire: The first prospect was a little-known man named Jim Stack, who had very large stock holdings in Quaker Oats. Biltz brought Stack up to Lake Tahoe, and put him up in the Brockway Hotel, planning to take him out to see some lakefront land the next morning.

"So what happens?" Biltz recalled fifty years later. "We get a snow-storm—about eight inches of snow—and we can't move. And we need this sale so bad. So what the hell are we going to do now? I thought, 'Well, by God, I can carry him over there,' because Jim had had a stroke and was partially paralyzed on the left side. I said, 'Jim, get up on my back. By God, we've come all this way together to see this property!' So I packed him over there, and packed him back. We sold him fifty thousand dollars' worth of property that day."

Biltz and his partners didn't stop with the land sales.

"We found that we had to go further than just to bring them in and drop them. So we had to start a construction company, to build houses in the manner that they wanted them built. We found servants for them; we catered to them in every possible way. I know with Jim Stack, I lived with him for six months, making him feel it was only advantageous to live in Nevada. Taking them shooting, fishing, with the result that these people became salesmen for us when they went back to Chicago or California or Oregon or wherever. We spent many an hour, day, week, and month, keeping them laughing, playing golf with them and letting them beat us."

Stack was soon followed by Max Fleischmann, heir to a yeast fortune, E. L. Cord, creator of a famous automobile, the family of newspaper publisher E. W. Scripps, Rex Bell and several other Hollywood stars, Cornelius Vanderbilt III, and at least seventy-five other millionaires.

Along the way, Biltz became a multi-millionaire himself. When *Fortune* magazine profiled him in 1954, the writer summarized the rewards Biltz had accumulated since his arrival in Reno in 1927: "He owns forty-four thousand acres along the Humboldt River and has federal grazing rights for an additional million acres. He runs some fourteen thousand head of cattle, leases eleven acres of ranch property in California, and owns virtually the entire

Max Fleischmann—who later gave millions to support museums, libraries, parks, clinics, and the unique Fleischmann Atmospherium Planetarium in Reno—provided twenty-five million dollars in grants to the University of Nevada system. "A millionaire doesn't deserve a damn bit of praise for using whatever money he has to help other people," he said, "but he deserves a lot of discredit if he doesn't."

shoreline of beautiful Donner Lake in the Sierra."

Biltz gained a reputation as a kingmaker, and by the time of his death in 1973 he was widely recognized as one of the most influential men in Nevada.

The Traveling Entertainers: Promoters like Norman Biltz made their fortunes by giving people what they wanted. One thing they always wanted was entertainment.

The love of show business was part of Nevada from the earliest days, when traveling tent shows brought banjo music, jokes and brief glimpses of female beauty to isolated mining camps. Then, at the height of the Comstock prosperity, Virginia City became the entertainment capital of the West.

Even San Francisco took a back seat in 1864 when the notorious Adah Isaacs Menken appeared in "Mazeppa" at Maguire's Opera House. Scandalous! New York audiences had already absorbed the initial shock when the daring actress, lashed to the back of an unsaddled horse, galloped across the stage wearing only pink tights that looked like nothing at all.

The *Gold Hill News* heralded her arrival on the Comstock:

> She has come! The Menken was aboard one of the pioneer coaches which reached Gold Hill this morning at half past eleven o'clock. She is decidedly a pretty little woman . . . She will doubtless draw large crowds in Virginia City with her *Mazeppa* and *French Spy* in which she excels any living actress.

"The Menken" scandalized and delighted Virginia City—but Mark Twain was bored.

A more matter-of-fact announcement in the *Daily Alta* remarked, "That the house will be crowded there can be little doubt. She is supported by Messrs. Booth, Mayo, Miss Sophia Edwin and the strength of the company."

Mark Twain of the *Territorial Enterprise* was unimpressed. He had seen the actress in an earlier performance in San Francisco and wrote, "Without any apparent reason for it, she carries on like a lunatic from the beginning of the act to the end of it."

His friend and fellow journalist, Dan De Quille, recalled Menken's later attempt to impress Mark Twain during a dinner party at the International Hotel. According to De Quille, the Menken thought herself a poet and novelist and wanted advice about her literary future.

"Mark disliked the Menken," De Quille wrote, "and would have avoided the arrangement that seated him by her side had it been possible. Mark...soon imagined a pressing engagement and begged to be excused."

Others in Virginia City were less resistant to her charms. At the end of her engagement at Maguire's Opera House, the city named a street for Menken and gave her a bullion bar worth two thousand dollars in exchange for a promise to return.

Maguire's wasn't the only theater in Virginia City. Tent shows had been popular with the miners even before the city was incorporated. As early as 1860, Sheriff William Henry Howard set up a wooden stage and called it *The Howard Theater*.

Tom Maguire, a San Francisco impresario, opened his opera house on D Street in Virginia City in 1863 and immediately started booking New York shows. If performances were sold out, seekers of diversion could find alternative entertainment at one of the other theaters. There was plenty of money on the Comstock and performers loved the excitement of traveling to the Wild West.

According to an anonymous historian, writing in a cooperative *WPA Guide to Nevada:* "At one time (in Virginia City) five companies were presenting the drama of tradition, from Shakespeare down, while six others were coining money with song and dance acts and acrobatic displays."

After twelve years in Virginia City, Maguire sold his theater. The buyer was John Piper, whose name soon was associated with top entertainment across the country and on both sides of the Atlantic. When the opera house burned down in 1875, Piper rebuilt it and gave it his name. After another fire in 1883, he moved to a different location, on B Street, and built a new theater.

Piper's Famous Opera House: Piper's Opera House became Nevada's Broadway. When Comstock millionaires wanted culture with a capital C, they invited friends to an evening at Piper's. Ornate posters outside the theater announced the names of famous players and singers, "recently arrived from London" or "acclaimed in New York."

In cultivated tones, the voices of Edwin Booth, Thomas R. Keene, Laurence Barrett and John McCullough brought Shakespearean drama to Piper's stage. Maude Adams packed the house. Enrico Caruso shook the ceiling with his powerful tenor.

Popular players like Frank Mayo and Joe Jefferson became "Davy Crockett" and "Rip Van Winkle" behind the footlights. When Lillie Langtry arrived from London with her song and dance act, curious crowds lined up to see the famous "Jersey Lily," a favorite mistress of England's King Edward VII.

For a while in the 1880s—before he went to New York to manage the Madison Square and Lyceum theaters—young David Belasco from San Francisco was Piper's stage manager. Later, through three decades, he produced a string of successes, including *Girl of the Golden West*. Long after his death, the producer's name is still in lights on the marquee of the Belasco Theater in Manhattan.

When Comstock fortunes dwindled, Nevada's entertainment headquarters moved to Reno. The little town on the Truckee had theaters, even when it was no more than a railroad link with Virginia City.

The town was just one year old when its first theater, Dyer's, opened in 1871. Flimsily built, Dyer's collapsed a few years later. Then Smith's Academy of Music became Reno's only showcase for traveling talent, until Hammond and Wilson's Theater joined the competition in 1889.

At the turn of the century, fans of melodrama flocked to Wheelman's Theater where Clara Kimball Young played ingenue parts, before she went to California to become a star of silent movies.

Reno's McKissick Opera House, opened in 1890, was the main Nevada stage until 1910 when U.S. Senator George S. Nixon built the big, new Majestic Theater. Five years later, the Rialto opened and started importing more headline entertainment.

When the Rialto became the Granada, Reno was the most popular theater town between New York and San Francisco. Big names like Otis Skinner, Jane Cowl and Minnie Maddern Fiske appeared on the Granada marquee. Railroads offered special Reno stop-over privileges to New York theater companies enroute to San Francisco.

The First World War brought an end to extravagant live productions. By 1920, Reno's big theaters were showing movies. All over the country, audiences lined up to see western films—and moviemakers found dramatic backgrounds in Nevada.

Comstock silver barons and their bejeweled companions watched world-famous entertainers on the stage of Piper's Opera House.

Goldwyn Discovers Nevada: When producer Sam Goldwyn wanted authentic background for an ambitious "super colossal" film in 1926, he sent director Henry King to search for a desert location. It had to look like California's Imperial Valley as it once was, before irrigation transformed it from desert into rich farmland.

The film was *The Winning of Barbara Worth*, based on a then-famous novel by Harold Bell Wright. The stars were Ronald Coleman and Vilma Banky, but a young Montana cowboy, in his first screen appearance, almost stole the show. His name was Gary Cooper.

King selected a spot in northern Nevada, near the Black Rock Desert, and there built a town large enough to accommodate three thousand people— and destined from the beginning to become a ghost town. At the suggestion of movie publicity people, the town was incorporated as "Barbara Worth, Nevada," and producer Goldwyn appointed King mayor.

Half a century later, Russell Nielsen recalled the creation of the short-lived town:

> A special train from Los Angeles carried crews to build a railroad spur and a headquarters site. Soon there was a sprawling tent city containing a mess hall, drug store, hotel, newspaper, bank, and theater. Wells were dug which fed a domestic water and sanitation system. Then there were refrigeration and electric lights.
>
> Sets were spotted over a 70-mile stretch to depict towns involved in a Colorado River flood which formed the Salton Sea. Shooting the scenes was difficult. Ground temperatures reached 130 degrees. Sandstorms were a daily occurrence, some so severe a person couldn't see across the 50-foot street.

After eight busy weeks of shooting, the cast and crew climbed aboard the train and "Barbara Worth, Nevada" was abandoned.

Now, Nielsen wrote in 1976, "There is only desert solitude where the once-busy film site lies beneath the sand. Occasionally, the wind blows the sand away from a relic of the past. Otherwise, there is nothing to show it once was the town of Barbara Worth."

The Presidential Fan: Film cowboys frequently raced across the Nevada desert during the late 1920s and the 1930s, but Reno's movie boom began with the appointment of John O. Moseley as president of the University of Nevada in 1944.

Moseley was "a gracious but ineffectual Texan" whose "administrative and intellectual talents were less than conspicuous," James Hulse wrote in his candid *The University of Nevada: A Centennial History*. The regents were so uncertain of his skill in dealing with the state legislature that they sent a substitute to Carson City to negotiate the budget.

But Moseley had no problems at all in dealing with 20th Century Fox or other film companies. He opened the campus to them, and their gratitude was reflected in an item in his *1946 Report of the President*:

"The 20th Century Fox Company gave one thousand dollars to be added to the 'President's Discretionary Fund' as a token of appreciation for the privilege of filming '*Margie*' on the University campus."

In 1947, the studio's gratitude increased by fifty percent. It donated fifteen hundred dollars in appreciation for Moseley's action in turning the campus over to the cast and crew of *An Apartment for Peggy*.

Joyce Laxalt, who was then Joyce Nielsen, remembers playing the part of a divorcée in one of the films made in Reno during this period. "I stood on the bridge and tossed my wedding ring into the Truckee," she recalls.

Marilyn Melton, then Marilyn Royle, was chosen as an extra in *Andy Hardy's Blonde Trouble*, starring young Mickey Rooney.

"Most of the time we just stood around in front of the Education Building, waiting to be told when to walk from Point A to Point B," she remembers. "Sometimes we'd repeat a scene over and over again, but we didn't mind. We were making $7.50 a day—-and that was big money in those days."

One faculty member, English professor Robert Gorrell, was chosen for a speaking part as a lawyer in *Captive City*, playing the scene with an actor named John Forsythe.

"It was his first film," Gorrell recalled, "and it was my last."

Although students were diverted by Moseley's ability to bring in stars such as Loretta Young, Jeanne Crain, Mickey Rooney and William Holden, the Board of Regents seemed less amused. After grumbling for months about the way the president spent his time, the board finally invited him to resign in 1949, and with some reluctance he took down the autographed photos of his favorite stars and departed.

During the 1950s, movie companies arrived and departed from Reno without arousing any special interest. But in 1960 the making of *The Misfits* brought other activities in the town to a near halt—including gambling at Harrah's.

This was Arthur Miller's first screenplay. He had written it specifically for Marilyn Monroe—just before the break-up of their marriage. Clark Gable seemed uncomfortable "surrounded by the new crop of actors, whose method he could not understand," one film critic observed. Director John Huston, who spent his evenings wandering from casino to casino, drinking steadily and

Apartment for Peggy was based on a real-life story by Barbara Gunn, then a student at the University of Oregon. It appeared first in *The Saturday Evening Post* in May 1948. The author sold film rights to Hollywood, but didn't see the movie until 1986, during a nostalgic film festival at the University of Nevada, Reno, where she had become State Extension Specialist in Human Development and Family Studies.

gambling wildly, openly displayed his disgust with Monroe, who never appeared before 10:30, an hour and a half behind her morning film call.

Memory of Marilyn. Seventeen years after the making of the film, Mark Curtis, vice president of Harrah's in charge of advertising and press relations, recalled one brief view of Marilyn:

> The company was shooting at Harrah's Club on Virginia Street. The scene had Marilyn in a conversation with Thelma Ritter by a bank of slot machines. The casino was cleared except for the crew and extras. I can't believe we did that— closed the casino for three days. But you have to understand that the whole town was overwhelmed by this picture, its stars and the glamour.
>
> I sat on a stool at a 21 table across from the pit where the scene was being set up. It was amazingly quiet considering all the activity—lights being placed, the crew running around, a crowd on the sidewalk. Marilyn was standing in the midst of the confusion, across from me, thirty or forty feet away. She could have been a waif who had wandered in off the street, or a hooker on the prowl. She was so alone . . . Her cheap dress for the scene was tight and thin, and in the warm morning she was cold. She hugged her arms around her.
>
> I watched her for a long time. Suddenly she turned and looked right at me. The vacant expression turned into a smile, but it wasn't a happy smile. More like a smile from a sick bed. Her mouth formed a "Hi." She was trying to communicate with the only one in the place who was thinking about her. She was hardly noticed by anyone else. She was like part of the equipment, something to be moved, set up, and eventually turned on. . . .

Marilyn Monroe and Clark Gable in Reno while filming *The Misfits*, 1960.

The Misfits turned out to be the last film made by Clark Gable, who died just eleven days after it was completed. A year and a half later, in June 1962, the *Nevada State Journal* carried a brief story:

> Hollywood (AP)—Marilyn Monroe is out of work today— fired by the same studio that made her a star. The sacking, which caught almost no one by surprise, came Friday only hours after Marilyn notified 20th Century-Fox that she was

"ready and eager to return to work Monday morning." But the studio wasn't impressed and called Lee Remick to take over. In another development, the studio announced it had begun action against Marilyn to recover five hundred thousand dollars allegedly lost as a result of the star's frequent absences from the set. . . .

The picture she was fired from was *Something's Got to Give*. She was never offered another screen role.

Marilyn Monroe and Frank Sinatra, rarely photographed together, were captured by Reno photographer Don Dondero in 1960.

The Parade of Stars: While *The Misfits* was being filmed in and around Reno, the town and its outskirts also provided backgrounds for episodes of a popular television series, *Route 66*. About the same time, producers of television commercials discovered ready-made sets in Nevada's deserts.

Moviemakers had used these desert backgrounds for years, since the earliest cowboy stars galloped through the sagebrush in the early 1920s. By 1965, producers of biblical epics knew exactly where to find a convincing Sea of Galilee close to home. When *The Greatest Story Ever Told* came to the screen, some Reno movie-goers recognized Pyramid Lake.

During the next thirty years, Reno saw plenty of movie and television people around town. John Wayne swaggered in to make *The Shootist* in 1975. Bette Midler arrived in 1981 to star in *Jinxed*. Clint Eastwood drew crowds in 1988 while filming *Pink Cadillac*. Tom Selleck was recognized by Reno fans while working in *An Innocent Man* in 1989. James Caan turned up in 1990 while playing the victim in Stephen King's *Misery*, filmed in nearby Genoa.

Now movies are big business in Nevada. By 1990, the State Motion Picture Division in Las Vegas reported that Nevada ranked fourth among all states in feature film production—behind only California, New York and Hawaii.

But most of the seven million visitors who swarm into Reno every year aren't thinking about possible glimpses of movie stars. What they've come to expect in Reno is live entertainment on big stages in casino showrooms. It's a tradition.

Those who remember the city in the 1950s and '60s will tell you they saw Jimmy Durante and Pearl Bailey at the Riverside and Liberace at the Mapes. They heard Andy Williams sing with Benny Goodman's orchestra and laughed through the evening when Milton Berle and Jack Benny came to town.

Nevada landscapes continue to provide locations for movies and television commercials in the 1990s. During the first year of the decade, the state collected nearly forty-six million dollars from such productions. Robert M. Hirsch, director of the Nevada State Motion Picture Division, says the major films made here are like cats with nine lives, moving from first-run theaters to television showings and then to video cassettes.

Some superstars played in Reno so often they seemed like homefolks. Frank Sinatra and his buddies knew the names of their favorite waiters. Bill Cosby, Debbie Reynolds, Rich Little and Jay Leno returned, year after year. Country music stars like Loretta Lynn, Kenny Rogers and Randy Travis played to record crowds.

Sammy Davis, Jr., who first appeared in Reno in 1930 as a child star at the old Club Fortune, made regular appearances at Harrah's for nearly thirty years. When he died in 1990, the casino renovated and renamed its Headliner Room, calling it Sammy's Showroom.

A collection of Sammy Davis memorabilia is displayed in a glass case at the entrance of Sammy's Showroom. His black derby hat, gold plated microphone and a single black patent leather dancing shoe—with a lifted heel, to make him look taller—share space with a gallery of photographs. A lettered text concludes with this tribute:

"At Harrah's in September 1988 he gave his last performance. This showroom, in which Sammy Davis, Jr. performed 440 times, is dedicated to his memory."

HEYDAY OF SUPERSTAR IS PAST shouted the headline above a Reno *Gazette-Journal* story about casino showrooms in the 1990s. Reporter Barbara Anderson explored the newspaper's files and recalled earlier days: "It wasn't unusual in the 1950s and '60s to have Sammy Davis, Jr., Wayne Newton and Liberace, as well as Frank Sinatra, Benny Goodman and Pearl Bailey playing showrooms in Reno and Tahoe. Their audiences were the rich and famous who were here to get divorced, married, or just to vacation."

Doubtful at first about the value of entertainers to casino owners, Bill Harrah (right) was converted by stars like Sammy Davis, Jr. Here he and Davis shake hands after agreeing to a million-dollar contract.

Politics, Nevada Style

"Being a cattle thief don't disqualify a man for anything political he may want in this state," H. M. Yerington, who was long active in Nevada political affairs, once wrote to a friend. "Really, from instances I have known . . . it adds to a man's standing in the community. . . ."

Senator Sharon's Fortune: There is no record that William Sharon, U.S. Senator from Nevada from 1874 to 1880, was ever accused of stealing cattle. It wouldn't have been worth his time, since he had found many other more profitable ways to build a fortune that made him the "second wealthiest man in California."

It might seem strange that he was identified with California although he represented Nevada in the Senate. But that is just one odd detail about one of the great scoundrels of the nineteenth century.

Sharon's life got off to a rocky start. He speculated recklessly in the great mining boom during the 1850s and early 1860s and unfortunately the mines he selected went broke as soon as the promoters had raked in all the cash they could from unwary investors.

By 1863, Sharon was reduced to living off a monthly allowance from William Ralston, another California speculator who had made better guesses.

Throughout his life, most people who knew Sharon well took a strong dislike to him. One historian later wrote, "It is probably impossible to find a kind word that was ever said about him."

Ralston, however, seems to have seen qualities in his protegé that were not visible to others. In addition to feeding and supporting him during his lean

Opposite page
Senator Key Pittman (right), a troubled figure in Nevada politics, gained the attention of such national leaders as President Franklin D. Roosevelt (center) and Vice President John Nance Garner (left) during the 1930s.

days, the wealthy banker sent Sharon to Virginia City in 1863 to open a branch of the powerful Bank of California.

That year marked the beginning of a near-depression in the Comstock mines, shortly before the discovery of the Big Bonanza. Mine owners, desperate for cash, were ready to pay premium rates for loans, and Sharon was ready to accommodate them. Setting interest rates at 24 percent a year (payable in monthly installments)—he was eager to consider any loan request he received.

When miners failed to make a monthly payment at these usurious rates—as most did—Sharon was equally eager to take over their working equipment. With plenty of cash, he was then able to dig deeper into the mountains and was able to turn mines that seemed worked out and worthless into very profitable ventures.

Sharon also added to his fortune with one project that was actually of great benefit to Reno. With Ralston and banker D. O. Mills he built the Virginia and Truckee railroad, which wound 1,575 feet down a mountain and connected Virginia City and Reno. This meant that the millions in silver ore from the Comstock was transported through the little town on the Truckee.

Naturally, Sharon arranged things so that he and his partners ended up with the enormous profits from the Virginia and Truckee, while most of the cost of construction was charged to two counties the railroad ran through.

In a few years Sharon and Ralston owned most of the mines of any value in the Comstock.

San Francisco banker William Ralston, above, sent his protegé, William Sharon, to Nevada to open a branch of the Bank of California.

Lucky Ralston's Bad Luck: Ralston, whose early speculations made him very rich, became a little wild in his later days. Among his many projects was the construction of two luxurious hotels in San Francisco—the Palace and the Grand. He also gambled heavily on developing a promising new mine that did not keep its promises, using money borrowed from his own bank (sometimes forgetting to record the loans).

He ended by taking a few too many chances, and the directors of the Bank of California realized one day that they had obligations totalling thirty million dollars and had just thirty thousand in cash in the till.

The directors—all of whom had grown rich under Ralston's leadership—forced him to resign. Despondent, Ralston strolled from the ornate bank building over to the north beach. His body was found floating in the bay later the same day.

A Short History of Reno

Sharon paid his respects to his benefactor that evening. Viewing the corpse at the morgue, he said to a fellow banker, "It's the best thing he could have done."

It did turn out to be the best thing for Sharon. Ralston, to the surprise of those who detested Sharon, left a statement naming him as Ralston's heir.

Without displaying excessive sorrow, he moved into a mansion Ralston had built, "and sent Mrs. Ralston and her family to what had been the servant's quarters," Gilman M. Ostrander reports in *Nevada: The Great Rotten Borough*. When she objected, he gave her just enough money to keep her quiet.

The Bank of California recovered from its temporary slump and many of the other wild Ralston ventures prospered. The once penniless Sharon found himself with a fortune of twenty-five million dollars.

As the millions poured in, Sharon decided to buy a seat in the United States Senate.

Although his home was in San Francisco, he apparently decided that it was easier to purchase the high honor in Carson City than in Sacramento.

William Sharon was one of the five multimillionaires who bought a U.S. Senate seat by bribing Nevada voters. Once he was elected, he rarely visited Washington and almost never spent a night in Nevada, since his favored mistress lived in a hotel he owned in San Francisco.

Senate Seats For Sale: The pattern for selecting senators from Nevada had been set by his predecessors. Since senators were then chosen by state legislatures—not by direct vote—if you wanted to be elected senator you had to begin by buying the votes of members of the Nevada state assembly and the state senate.

This could be expensive, since many state senators and assemblymen had to buy votes themselves to gain their own seats in the legislature. The going price for the support of a Nevada voter varied from year to year, and from one district to another, but the bidding rose steadily during this period—from around fifteen to forty dollars, and then to eighty dollars a vote. (Some said the higher bid was necessary because voters disliked Sharon so much that they had upped their price.)

Of course, not all voters were for sale, regardless of the price offered, but enough were to make this an expensive transaction. The cost of electing a U.S. senator in Nevada during the 1870s through the 1890s was rarely less than two hundred and fifty thousand dollars, and could rise to eight hundred thousand or more if you were both very rich and widely despised.

A few of the unbought legislators were a bit disturbed by the fact that the candidate for senator had been living in San Francisco for the past three years

"Throughout his business career, William Ralston persisted in the belief that there was honor among thieves, a beguiling streak of guilelessness that ultimately did him in. It was not until the day of his death that he learned otherwise. . . ."—*Nevada: The Great Rotten Borough*

and rarely visited Nevada, except on this recent vote-buying mission. One of them introduced a resolution expressing concern over the carpetbag candidate, but this was ruled "out of order" in the state assembly and tabled in the state senate. The vote followed quickly, and few seemed surprised at Sharon's triumph.

Although he had gone to much trouble and expense to win a seat in the U.S. Senate, Sharon showed little inclination to sit in it once he was elected. His achievements over the next six years were summarized by Nevada historian Russell Elliott:

> Sharon's record in the United States Senate is one of the worst in the history of that legislative body. His record of inaction is unbelievable. He was seated at only five sessions and was recorded on less than one percent of the roll calls. He never introduced a bill and if he spoke on one it is not recorded . . . His absences from Washington were exceeded only by those from the state he was supposed to represent; his only visits to Nevada during his incumbency in the Senate came while passing through the state on his way to or from the east.

Another commentator explains that Sharon's reluctance to spend much time in Washington was traceable to his preference for the company of one of his mistresses, who lived in the Hotel Grand in San Francisco and made frequent visits to his suite in the Palace. (A second-story walkway leading from the Grand to the Palace made her journeys at late hours simpler.) This particular mistress—one of several on his payroll—later proved that Sharon had written out a "marriage contract" to overcome her feelings that she might be doing something immoral.

Since he wouldn't acknowledge the marriage, the mistress took the unusual step of suing him for divorce to prove that she had been his wife. Suits and countersuits kept the courts of California busy for years, led to the murder of the mistress's second husband, and were still unsettled when Sharon died, unmourned by Nevada voters.

Many of the early Nevada senators spent part of their time working for the railroad, since much of the money the candidates spent to buy votes came from the Central Pacific or the Virginia & Truckee. When Senator William M. Stewart needed a little extra cash, he wrote to a V&T officer: "It occurred to me that the Virginia & Truckee Railroad Company might make me an officer or employee. . . . Why could I not be your attorney? I am a pretty good lawyer and you couldn't get a cheaper one under these circumstances. Let me know if you can't figure out so that what little salary I get won't all be used up in traveling expenses. . . ."

Winning the Graveyard Vote: A later refinement in Nevada elections was the custom of copying names from gravestones, thus allowing the honored dead to join in electing officials. This was especially common in Storey County (where the Comstock Lode was located). The master of this method of increasing participation in civic affairs was Billy

Sharon, nephew of Senator Sharon.

A newspaperman named Sam Davis celebrated the contributions by the senator and his nephew to Storey County election traditions in "Lines to a Comstock Graveyard":

> On yonder hillside, bleak and barren,
> Lies many a friend of William Sharon,
> Who in election's hurly-burly,
> Voted often, voted early.
> But since old Sharon went to glory
> The younger Billy bosses Storey,
> And at his beck those sons of witches
> Rise, to vote without their britches.
> To take a hand in the election
> And bustle back without detection.
> As we recall those mem'ries hoary,
> Let's bless the graveyard vote of Storey.

By 1880 even Nevada legislators were disenchanted with the absentee senator and waited to see who else would show up to bid for their votes for the term beginning in 1881.

It turned out to be a good year for them. First James G. Fair, one of the "Big Four" owners of the Big Bonanza, decided that the title of senator was worth at least half a million dollars, and was ready to go higher if necessary. The fact that he was almost as widely detested in Nevada as Sharon again raised the price for each purchased vote.

Fair sent representatives, called "sack bearers," into every Nevada county. These gentlemen were empowered to reach into their sacks and pay voters forty to eighty dollars each to vote for legislators pledged to elect Fair to the Senate. According to H. M. Yerington, Fair's men also "naturalized" some floating French and Italian immigrants who had not gotten around to applying for U.S. citizenship so they would also have a chance to express their preferences for the legislature.

It appeared that the election had been properly bought and paid for, but suddenly the legislators were provided with a second opportunity to improve their fortunes. Adolph Sutro—builder of the famous Sutro Tunnel in Virginia City—decided to try again for the Senate after two earlier unsuccessful attempts.

Sutro first sent an agent to Nevada to persuade a majority of the members

Collis P. Huntington, one of the Big Four who built the Central Pacific, grew very fond of the helpful Senator Stewart. Stewart "has always stood by us," Huntington wrote to one of his partners. "He is peculiar, but thoroughly honest, and will bear no dictation." Then he added: "But I know he must live, and we must fix it so that he can make one or two hundred thousand dollars. It is to our interest, and I think his right."

Tunnel builder Adolph Sutro spent a quarter of a million dollars on the purchase of a U.S. Senate seat, but was outbid by one of the bonanza multimillionaires.

of the legislature to switch their votes from Fair to him. Before the agent could arrange to pay off a sufficient number of the legislators, Fair bought *him* off.

His trust in human beings somewhat reduced by this act of perfidy, Sutro made the journey to Carson City himself and checked into the Ormsby House, not far from the state capitol. He let the word get around that he'd be happy to meet with the people's representatives and that he had enough cash with him to make the meetings worthwhile.

"At one point Sutro allegedly had thirty-five members of the legislature willing to renege on their pledges to Fair if some legitimate reason for doing so could be found," Russell Elliott reports. The legislators were looking for "moral grounds" for changing their votes after accepting Fair's money.

Sutro then came up with an elaborate scheme. He would accuse several of the legislators who insisted on remaining true to their pledges to Fair of buying votes for their election. That was easy enough to prove, since it had become an almost universal practice, but there was one problem: Warrants for the arrest of these corrupt legislators had to be sworn out in the presence of some official who was authorized to handle such a complaint.

"Fair's managers had learned of Sutro's scheme," Gilman M. Ostrander writes, "and had taken all such officials into hiding."

Recognizing that he was up against someone even more corrupt than himself, Sutro watched the disloyal legislators who had cost him something around $250,000 cast their votes for the man who had first purchased them. Fair was elected senator with fifty-two votes out of seventy-three. Sutro's name wasn't even mentioned on the floor of the state assembly or the senate.

Five multimillionaires bought seats in the U.S. Senate by bribing Nevada voters and Nevada legislators between 1872 and 1912.

One of them—Francis G. Newlands—actually turned out to be an effective senator, with one major blind spot.

Although he was the son-in-law of the notorious William Sharon, and inheritor of much of Sharon's wealth, Newlands gained a reputation as a reformer. He "believed that the Federal government should be a positive force in the economic and social welfare of the people," Russell Elliott wrote. He supported unions, tried to introduce national regulation to bring about unified control of the railroads, and was an outstanding early conservationist. Some of his ideas were considered dangerously radical by traditionalists in the Senate.

His most notable achievement was the sponsorship of the Newlands Reclamation Act of 1902, which reclaimed thousands of acres of desert land in Nevada and other western states.

Francis G. Newlands was the only one of the enormously wealthy early U.S. senators from Nevada who actually served with distinction.

Newlands's limitations were demonstrated in statements he made about the Fifteenth Amendment, which enfranchised the slaves. Newlands called for the repeal of that amendment and said blacks should be denied the right to vote.

The Politician's Friend: By 1910, it was no longer essential to be a multimillionaire to be elected senator from Nevada. It did help if you had rich and powerful friends—especially one named George Wingfield.

Wingfield, later an eminent citizen of Reno, was a penniless gambler when he arrived in the remote town of Tonopah, Nevada, in 1902. He quickly found a job as a dealer at the Tonopah Club, and when not dealing cards he was playing them. He was particularly good at a rather tricky game called faro, and one day had a lucky run which left him with winnings of twenty-two hundred dollars. That changed his life—and changed political life in Nevada for a generation.

That twenty-two-hundred-dollar win gave Wingfield the money he needed to take over the gambling operations in the club, in partnership with another man. He used his profits (of about two hundred thousand dollars a year) to buy the richest mining properties in the Tonopah-Goldfield region.

He had a different partner in this venture—a very successful banker named George Nixon—and they shared with Bernard Baruch in the twenty-nine million dollars in dividends paid by the Goldfield Consolidated Mining Company.

As the millions piled up, Nixon decided he would like to have the U.S. Senate seat that had been occupied by four earlier Nevada multimillionaires. He won it in 1905, and served "with that lack of distinction which was traditional among Nevada senators," Gilman Ostrander observes.

When Nixon died in 1912, Wingfield took control of the banks he had established in Tonopah, Carson City, Winnemucca and Reno. Wingfield also became the owner of hotels and cattle ranches, and had a secret interest in the largest brothel in the state and the most luxurious of the illegal gambling clubs.

But he is remembered best for something else.

His office—Room 201 in the Reno National Bank Building—was widely recognized as "the real capital of Nevada." Wingfield headed the state Republican party, and a lawyer who worked for him and occupied an adjoining office headed the Democratic party. If you wanted a favor from either party, you

Nevadans grew so accustomed to corrupt politicians that some expressed surprise when an officeholder did not grow wealthier through secret deals. "Tasker Oddie's tour of duty in the state house is testimony either to his incorruptibility or to the insignificance of the governorship, for he left office as poor as when he entered it," one historian observed. He was often deeply in debt, and creditors who had been dunning him for years assumed that once he was elected governor he would have free access to the state treasury. One wrote: "You have frequently written us that you were going to do something when you got on your feet, and that was six years ago. Surely it is not possible that you have not made a fortune. . . ."

could reach the party boss by telephoning the same number: 4111.

Wingfield's power was reflected in a letter one experienced political figure, Thomas W. Miller, wrote to Tasker Oddie, when Oddie was beginning a campaign for the U.S. Senate:

> You have made mistakes in your past political performances, the same as all of us, and I think one of your greatest faults is not taking advice as to the policies to be followed from those of your friends who know how to give advice in matters political. If nominated, I would place myself absolutely in the hands of your State Committee or in Wingfield, and confer with them and follow along the lines suggested by them. . . .

Oddie followed Miller's advice, served two undistinguished terms in the U.S. Senate, and ended with the usual tribute from his fellow citizens—a boulevard named in his honor which carries Renoites past trailer parks, parking lots, and shopping centers to the neighboring city of Sparks.

Wingfield's "bipartisan machine" arranged matters so the state sent one Democratic senator and one Republican senator to Washington during the 1920s and into the 1930s.

Key Pittman's extraordinary political success was not enough to free him from his compulsive, erratic behavior, including his habit of firing at the ceilings of restaurants when he felt the service was too slow.

The Troubled Senator: The first of these senators to gain international attention was Key Pittman, a strange, tortured man who served five terms and was on his way to his sixth when he died, mysteriously, in 1940.

Pittman was easily bored, and as a young lawyer he hurried off to join the Klondike gold rush. Arriving late, he made no fortune there, but he did get a chance to practice mining law, and found a wife in Alaska. After returning to the U.S. he heard of the gold and silver discoveries in Tonopah and decided to set up his practice in that remote and dusty little town.

After his first look at Nevada he wrote to his wife, Mimosa, about the attractions of Tonopah and his plans for the future:

> I am thinking of making our home in Nevada and growing up with the country. I see many opportunities here both in law, mines, and politics. I feel very confident that I will be employed in most of the large suits and the boys are even now talking of running me for the legislature.

He didn't make it to the legislature but after a few unsuccessful political campaigns he was elected senator in 1912, and re-elected every six years for the rest of his life. He became chairman of the Senate Foreign Relations Committee and a friend—or at least a valuable political supporter—of President Franklin D. Roosevelt.

His public success did not conceal his private pain. He gained a reputation as a wild man who carried a pearl-handled pistol, and occasionally fired at the ceiling of a restaurant in Washington when annoyed by the slow service. His first act as chairman of the foreign relations committee was to install a well-stocked bar.

He was capable of brutally frank self-analysis. His complex problems surface in many of his letters to his wife, including one written when he was already a widely-known and very influential member of the Senate:

> You will try and analyze my life with me? I was and had been for years a periodical drunkard. For months my mind worked ceaselessly, and with a feverish energy.... Every act was marked by patience and clarity—Then came the reaction ... the breaking of the other chain.... A mania seized me, you cannot understand it, and no one can explain—and my growing desire was to escape from myself, from my thoughts, from my will. All of the savage in man asserted itself in me. I longed for, and nothing satisfied me but the most intense excitement—I longed to murder, kill and howl with delight at the sound of death dealing instruments and the sight of human blood.

As Betty Glad, author of *Key Pittman: The Tragedy of a Senate Insider*, observes: "It was almost as if there were two Key Pittmans—the everyday, functioning, careful, rational 'Key Pittman' who learned his role as a Senate insider—and another basic self always at war with the everyday self and sometimes overwhelming it." His wife's "coldness, her refusal to give him the admiration and support he needed . . . helped trigger his recurrent rages," Glad says.

Sometimes Pittman's wilder impulses became dominant when he was under close observation by many people—including strangers who knew little about his accomplishments.

In *Nevada: The Great Rotten Borough*, Ostrander focuses on one of these periods. Pittman, then chairman of the powerful Senate Foreign Relations Committee, went to England as a U.S. representative at the London Economic Conference of 1933.

"Arriving in England, Pittman got drunk and stayed that way through

"Key Pittman won the Democratic nomination for Senator at the poker table," Gilman M. Ostrander reports in *Nevada: The Great Rotten Borough*. "On the night of the famous Johnson-Jeffries fight, staged in Reno, Pittman won $5,000 against other members of the Democratic State Central Committee. Already clearly eligible for the nomination, he pushed his easy money across the table and offered it for what he wanted and closed the deal."

much of the conference," Ostrander reports. "He had brought his gun with him, and at times, when he was drinking, he would let his spirits loose by popping out the London streetlights with his six-shooter. He had also brought a bowie knife, and when one technical advisor gave him trouble . . . Pittman took after him with his knife and chased him through the corridors of the Claridge Hotel."

One member of the delegation recalled a day when the distinguished senator was "completely out of working order." The evening before, "he had entertained two 'ladies' who were later ejected by the hotel. . . ."

Pittman arrived forty-five minutes late for the important international meeting, Ostrander reports, "just as a hastily chosen substitute was preparing to state his proposal. After Pittman introduced it for consideration, he continued with a rambling speech which was characterized as 'an utter disgrace.'"

As he neared the end of his fifth term, Pittman "must have known that his death was approaching," Ostrander reports. "He grew thinner and weaker and remained drunk for longer periods; also, he began to make maudlin and irresponsible statements."

But he'd gotten into the habit of running for office every six years, so he returned to Nevada to campaign during the fall of 1940.

On November 1, 1940, he disappeared from public view. The election was still five days away, and reporters who had been following him had noticed that he had become very thin, almost gaunt, and seemed under great strain.

Despite his obvious ill-health, it seemed almost certain that he was about to win his sixth term in the Senate. But candidates in Nevada have learned to expect upsets, and many keep speaking to any potential voter who will listen until the polls open.

A political ally reported to Senator Pat McCarran in 1940: "Senator Key Pittman is touring the state and it looks more or less good for him, but if he continues to try to drink the entire supply of John Barleycorn and keeps making a fool out of himself, no one can tell what will happen. . . ."

Senator on Ice: One political reporter, it was rumored later, asked one of Pittman's handlers why the senator was making no campaign appearances in this important final week. The handler replied: "We're keeping him on ice." This may account for a bizarre tale that was widely repeated in the state after the election.

Pittman died, according to the official records, on November 10, 1940, in a Reno hospital. This was four days after his overwhelming re-election to the Senate.

The widely circulated tale was that he had actually died in a hotel room "a few days before the election," and that his handlers, who feared that voters would switch over to his Republican opponent if they knew Pittman was dead, came up with a scheme to conceal that fact. The authors of *The Green Felt Jungle*—Las Vegas journalists Ed Reid and Ovid Demaris—stated flatly:

> It seems that Pittman died in November, 1940, just a few days before the election. Zealous Democrats, who knew that Pittman's opponent would be elected automatically if his death were announced before the voting took place, concealed the Senator's body in a bathtub in the Mizpah Hotel in Tonopah and covered it with cracked ice to preserve it.

Almost all historians consider the report false—but this account of Pittman's final exit has become one of the lasting legends of Nevada politics. And the fact that many people take it seriously indicates that Nevadans' regard for politicians hasn't changed much since Mark Twain lampooned the Territorial Legislature while working on the *Territorial Enterprise*.

In *Roughing It*, Twain set the tone that is still used by many Nevadans in commenting on their politicians:

> That was a fine collection of sovereigns, that first Nevada legislature. They levied taxes to the amount of thirty or forty thousand dollars and ordered expenditures to the extent of about a million. . . . The legislature sat sixty days, and passed private toll-road franchises all the time. When they adjourned it was estimated that every citizen owned about three franchises, and it was believed that unless Congress gave the territory another degree of longitude there would not be room enough to accommodate all the toll-roads. The ends of them were hanging over the boundary everywhere like a fringe. . . .

Later, journalist Lucius Beebe, who revived the *Enterprise* in the 1950s, echoed the same sentiment. He offered a suggestion for a change in the meeting time of the "bicameral zoo"—his affectionate name the Nevada State Legislature. Instead of meeting every second year for sixty days, Beebe proposed, it should meet every twenty years for five minutes.

"The damage to everyone they could do in even the minimum period would take sane and industrious citizens two decades to repair," he wrote.

The Well-Remembered Scalawags: During its first century and a quarter, the city of Reno and the state of Nevada have had some sane and honest public officials, ranging from city councilman and mayor

Nevada's not the greatest state
And if it ever hopes
To be among the best ones
Let women have the votes

This anonymous doggerel appeared in publications advocating women's suffrage in Nevada in 1913. Anne Martin led the campaign, traveling more than 6,000 miles by stagecoach, on horseback, by automobile, and on foot, sometimes "lowering herself by windlass into the mines by a bucket." "I believe she could address every voter by his first name," said one of the women working with her. In November, 1914, her long campaign ended, with 10,936 in favor of votes for women, 7,158 against.

to governor and U.S. senator.

These for the most part have been recognized briefly for their virtues and soon forgotten. The politicians who seem to live longest in the memory of most Nevadans are the clowns Mark Twain wrote about and the scoundrels and scalawags who succeeded them. Fortunately, there has never been a shortage of these figures during any decade in the state's history.

In his oral history, *Seventy Years of Griping: Newspapers, Politics, Government,* Nevada newspaperman John R. McCloskey offered this view of the state's voters: ". . . the public doesn't like the kind of politician that tells 'em the truth all the time."

In *Dateline Reno*, photographer Don Dondero's collection of celebrity photos includes four presidents of the United States. *Clockwise:* John F. Kennedy admires a beauty pageant winner; Lyndon B. Johnson campaigns in Reno; Reno author Robert Laxalt, center, watches as Richard M. Nixon meets other Nevadans; Ronald Reagan greets a lunchtime crowd.

IN FAIRNESS TO ALL

DEALER MAY INSIST ON THE CATCHING OF DICE IN
OPEN HAND, AND BOTH DICE HITTING END OF TABLE OR
SHOOTER TO BE PASSED BY THE DEALER – DICE STOPPING
ON FOUR OR MORE CHIPS OR DOLLARS-NO DICE –
DEALER MAY CALL NO DICE AT ANY TIME – ALL BETS
MUST BE PLACED BEFORE DICE ROLLED

NO CALL BETS ACCEPTED
HIGHER LIMITS BY REQUEST

Strangers Who Changed a City

7

Two strangers arrived in Reno during the 1930s with absolutely nothing in common except an interest in how to draw ordinary people into gambling parlors. By the end of the 1940s they had changed the town forever.

A   **Long Road to Reno:** One of the new arrivals took a long, round-about road before reaching Reno. Raymond I. Smith was the son of a Vermont farmer. His father died when Raymond was seven, and he decided early that he had no interest in trying to survive by helping his mother cultivate a poor, rocky farm. He went out searching for another way to make a living.

Before he reached his teens, Raymond discovered that Vermonters could be persuaded to risk some of their hard-earned nickels and dimes at county fairs if they stood a chance of winning a prize. The prize didn't have to amount to much—a cheap pocket knife was enough. And the rare winners were usually ready to sell the knife back for less than its cost. That made it possible for the operator to continue his game without investing much in prizes.

By offering prizes only in merchandise—not money—the operators of these games stayed just within the law, and no one seemed to worry about the second stage of the transaction, when the operator bought the knife back, thus effectively offering a cash prize.

Early in his wanderings young Smith was helping operate one of those games. It wasn't an easy life, but it offered him a chance to escape from the lonely farm and to see the sights at county fairs across the state. The hours were long, with no time to spare for school, so his formal education ended at

Opposite page
"Pappy" Smith (the gray haired man wearing glasses) presides over a busy gambling table at Harolds Club.

the age of seven.

From these early experiences, Smith began to recognize the strong attraction gambling held for ordinary people. They were ready to take a chance at a county fair, surrounded by their fellow farmers, but would never think of going into a gambling hall. This discovery changed Smith's life and later helped shape the lives of thousands of people living far across the continent from Vermont.

When he was 19, Raymond married a girl of 16, and at first she accompanied him on his journeys in search of Vermont farmers who were ready to take a chance on the wheel. In dealing with gamblers, Raymond was an easy-going, smiling man, but his wife soon became aware of the darker side of his character. Raymond could be cold and uncaring in his relationship with his young wife and his sons. His hard, lonely boyhood produced a tough, undemonstrative, self-sufficient man— "a perfect symbol of the rocky Vermont soil that spawned him," as his son Harold later wrote.

Raymond I. ("Pappy") Smith was more at ease dealing with the hard-luck stories of gamblers who came to Harolds Club than he was in his relationship with his wife and his sons.

Smith was often on the road, and after the two children were born his wife and his sons lived on very little money in a series of drab houses or rooms. In one of the temporary dwellings, Harold and his older brother Raymond slept in a tiny closet that had once been a butler's pantry—with no light.

During one of the many periods of separation, Harold recalls, he saw his mother "kiss a man who was not my father," and sensed the deep alienation between his parents.

He was then eight years old.

"I remember the moment as though it were only five minutes ago," Harold Smith wrote decades later. "I walked in from the hallway and he was kissing her ardently, right there in our home, and Mama didn't protest. She saw me. She kissed him back hard, on the lips. At eight years of age you react more from sensation than from judgment. I felt an agony of protest, a helplessness so deep I was limp."

A few days later, when Harold Smith awoke with a choking chest cold and called for his mother, he looked up and saw his father enter the room. Raymond Smith told Harold that his mother left during the night. "Blown town," was the expression Harold Smith remembered his father using.

Fighting back the terror in his chest and trying to be manly, Harold asked his father what he should do for his cold. Without showing much interest, his father told him to take some cough drops. "So I did."

His parents were divorced not long after that, and the two boys spent most of their time wandering from city to city with their mother, who remarried three times. When Harold was 17, he and his brother Raymond, Jr., received a call. Their father was running some games of chance at an amusement park called Chutes-at-the-Beach near San Francisco, and wanted the two boys to come out to work in these concessions.

Harold remembers the years that followed as a time when he was daily subjected to his father's stern orders and his impatience. One day when not enough of the visitors to the amusement park were stopping to bet a dime that they could knock over bottles by tossing a baseball, his father said critically: "They're walkin' by you!" And then he gave his orders: ". . . Get thirty feet out front and direct the traffic to your stand!"

Soon, Harold Smith recalls, he learned to "practically shove tickets into people's hands," hoping to impress his father, but he cannot remember his father expressing approval or thanking him.

T he Perils of Bingo: In 1935, Attorney General Earl Warren decided to save California from the unwholesome effects of bingo and penny roulette, and the Smiths found themselves facing a five-hundred-dollar fine and ninety-day suspended sentences for operating a bingo parlor in Modesto.

Disturbed by this puritanical campaign, Raymond I. Smith sent Harold to Reno, where gambling had recently been legalized.

Harold wasn't much impressed by his first sight of the town.

"There weren't any neons in the biggest little city then," he wrote in his autobiography, *I Want to Quit Winners*. "A high-rolling player would have got pretty sleepy action. I strolled into one club and tried a twenty-five-dollar bet on the crap table. I threw a seven and when the dealer paid me I let the fifty dollars ride.

"'You can't do that,' the dealer said huffily. 'The house limit's twenty-five.'

"A tinhorn town!" Harold remembered thinking. "*And this is legalized gambling!*"

Even though Harold had strong reservations about what he had seen in Reno, he and his father and brother decided to give the town a try. (Later Raymond I. Smith described his life-long motivation, explaining his nomadic existence: "I made up my mind early to find the place where the most money was changing hands fastest.")

Harold found a dingy little bingo parlor on South Virginia Street—"one

Harold Smith tries to interest a showgirl in his autobiography, *I Want to Quit Winners*. The title turned out to be ironic, since he lived out his last days on a small "spend-thrift" allowance from his attorney and a $317 per month Social Security payment after losing a fortune gambling at other casinos.

long room twenty-five by one hundred and twenty-five feet in a block close enough to the railroad tracks to be almost Skid Road."

On February 23, 1936, they opened a place they'd decided to call Harolds Club (without an apostrophe). It was Harold Smith's twenty-sixth birthday. Everything was about to change—for the wandering Smiths and for Reno.

The Mouse Game: Not long after Harolds Club opened, a stranger appeared with an idea that was new to Raymond Smith. It was called the mouse game, and it gained the club its first national attention.

"The mouse game is actually a form of roulette using a live mouse as the ball," Harold Smith later recalled. "The creature is placed in a box on a table top in which there are numbered holes large enough for him to crawl into. Each hole is numbered—ours ran from 1 to 50—and the player places his bet on the number he thinks the mouse will choose."

When the box is lifted to turn the mouse loose, everyone waits to see what hole he will go down. A box is placed under the table to catch the mouse after he chooses one of the numbered holes and disappears.

Harold Smith, who was out of town the day the stranger approached his father with the idea, had seen the mouse game before, and he knew there were two serious problems with it. One was the possibility of trickery by the opera-

Reno photographer Don Dondero encouraged a tamed white mouse to re-enact Harolds Club's famous "Mouse Game."

A Short History of Reno

tor of the game. Since a mouse will react almost immediately to any sharp noise and look for a place to escape, a dishonest operator of the mouse game only had to wait until the mouse was near a couple of numbers on which no player had bet, then shout something to the players, and the frightened mouse would dash down one of those nearby holes, saving the owner a pay-off on the game.

Harold Smith also realized that it wouldn't take players too long to recognize the possibilities in the game. Someone could bet heavily on two or three numbers, then startle the mouse with a sudden sound or a sudden motion when he was near one of those holes, causing him to scamper down.

Because of these invitations to cheaters, Harold Smith persuaded his father to say a reluctant farewell to the mouse game operator at the end of the first week. But before the new attraction was dropped, freelance news photographers had recorded the mouse's journey across the table top, and for years afterward visitors to Reno came into Harolds Club hoping to observe the famous mouse.

Harold Smith (right) poses stiffly with a security guard during the days of great prosperity at Harolds Club, then the best-known casino in the world. The club was later sold to Howard Hughes.

Harolds Club or Bust: The club became more famous during World War II, when soldiers, sailors and marines came into Reno on leave from western military bases and airfields. A vice president of Harolds Club came up with the slogan "Harolds Club or Bust" and a drawing of a covered wagon. Many young servicemen, impressed by Raymond I. ("Pappy") Smith's hospitable reception during their visits to Reno, began displaying the drawing and those four words wherever they traveled around the world. The slogan soon appeared in Europe, Asia, North Africa, Australia, and finally in Antarctica (with an arrow pointing toward Nevada and the distance indicated: "8,452 Miles to Harolds Club").

But the Smiths did not depend on servicemen alone to carry the message. After first studying the highway networks carefully, they erected twenty-three hundred signs on the busiest roads across the country—rivaling Burma Shave in the number of reminders to travelers.

"Pappy" occasionally took a gambler who had lost everything at the Harolds Club tables over to the nearby Greyhound bus station and bought him a one-way ticket home. Later, according to Lester Kofoed, who worked closely with the Smiths for years, he would quietly advance an unlucky gambler a month's rent, or give him fifty or a hundred dollars to get through to the next payday after a bad run at the club.

Officer in Trouble: One day a young lieutenant came into Harolds Club to ask for help. He discussed his problem with one of the dealers, who suggested that he go to see Mr. Smith. Gradually the full story emerged:

The lieutenant was in charge of the commissary at Stead Air Base, which was located about nine miles from Reno. He had come into town with about twenty-five hundred that belonged to the base commissary, hoping to win enough to replace the money he had taken and to have a couple of thousand left over to cover some of his personal bills. He had ended by losing it all.

"Do you have a family?" Smith asked him.

"Yes," the lieutenant said. "A wife and two children."

"What'll happen when the commanding officer discovers what you've done?" Smith asked.

"I'll be busted to private," the lieutenant said, "and given a dishonorable discharge."

Leslie Kofoed observed what happened next:

"Pappy investigated around the club and found that the man had been in there (in uniform), and that he had gambled," Kofoed recalled. "Pappy then asked the lieutenant if he had spent all of the money at Harolds Club, and he said: 'Lord, no.' He'd been in every club and casino and hotel in town, he said, and tried them all, and didn't have any luck at any of them.

"Despite that fact, and without any way of knowing how much money the lieutenant had lost in Harolds Club, Mr. Smith reimbursed him the full twenty-five hundred, but with the understanding that he would never gamble again as long as he lived."

Kofoed said that in one year Pappy Smith gave at least three hundred and fifty thousand dollars to gamblers who had lost everything. The amounts given to most of the losing gamblers were small—five or ten dollars to almost anyone who approached him with a hard-luck story—but from time to time Smith would hand out far more.

"Pappy" Smith's most important contribution to opening the doors of a gambling establishment to millions may be traced to a seemingly unimportant episode.

Harold Smith recalls the event:

"We didn't have lady customers when we first opened Harolds Club. We didn't have too many customers of any sex and we couldn't go out on the street and drag them in. One day as Daddy stood near the doorway, a woman came in, took two or three hesitant steps toward the first game and stopped

Pappy Smith would sometimes walk up to a 21 table and say to the dealer, "Give me that deck. I want to deal a sucker hand." Then he would deal himself five or six cards, making certain he would go bust by going over 21. Then he'd pay everybody off— sometimes doubling or tripling their bets.

A Short History of Reno

short. 'There are no women here!' she almost shrieked as she fled.

"Out of that episode, Daddy got the idea of lady dealers at our tables. Soon afterwards *The Saturday Evening Post* published a story on our lady dealers. That gave us the publicity break we needed and overnight the atmosphere of the club was changed by the presence of women at our tables."

During Pappy Smith's first two or three years in Reno, others in the gambling business "laughed at him," Silvio Petricianni, son of the operator of the old Palace Club, recalled years later. "Nobody thought he would get as big as he did. They thought he was crazy—an old carnival man."

They kept waiting for him to go broke, because of his handing out cash to gamblers in trouble and his disorganized way of operating his club.

Petricianni remembers trying to warn his father and another experienced casino operator, Jack Sullivan, that they were underestimating the Smiths.

"You know," young Petricianni told them, "you people sit here on Center Street bickering back and forth, and you're watching someone grow strong on Virginia Street and it's going to break you both."

Sullivan reached over and patted Petricianni on the face.

"It's all right, my boy," Sullivan said. "There's plenty of business for everybody."

A few years later, the Palace Club was torn down. The site it had occupied for years became a parking lot for buses bringing gamblers to Harrah's Club.

"The Smiths were being stolen blind, and didn't know it," an advertising man who worked for Pappy said in his oral history. "There was more stuff goin' out the back door than in the front door."

Expanding his bingo club in 1942, Bill Harrah added a 21 game, 20 slot machines, and a craps table (shown at left).

Tom Wilson, who handled much of the advertising for Harolds Club, said the club's extraordinary success in the 1930s and 1940s was traceable to "Pappy" Smith's skill in dealing with both players and employees.

"When Raymond I. was in full form," Wilson said, "he would go through the club, doubling people's bets (so winners would be paid twice as much if they were lucky, but lose no more than they had already bet) buying them drinks, slapping 'em on the back, cracking real corny jokes."

He was equally relaxed with his employees, Wilson recalled. "It was a warm, friendly, hilarious place. Nobody could touch him."

"Pappy" himself told of a middle-aged couple who came by to thank him before returning to California. The husband said to him, "We'd rather lose to you than to win from them other bastards."

From Venice to Reno: In the 1920s, while Raymond I. Smith was scratching out a living in amusement parks and at county fairs, John Harrah was conducting a very successful law practice in Venice, California, and serving a term as mayor of the city.

Harrah had invested in about forty business and residential properties, and he and his family lived very comfortably during the great boom.

John Harrah enjoyed luxuries himself, and passed along a taste for easy living to his son, Bill. When Bill asked his father for a Ranger motorbike, John Harrah said: "Anything you want that I can afford and your friends have, you can have." He explained that he didn't want Bill to buy something so expensive that it would arouse the envy of his friends.

The 1929 Wall Street crash first affected John Harrah's law practice, then led to the loss of the houses and almost all of the business structures he had invested in during the good years.

"A fifty thousand dollar piece of property with its twenty-five thousand dollar mortgage became a fifteen-thousand dollar piece of property with a twenty-five thousand dollar mortgage," Bill Harrah recalled.

Because he'd mortgaged everything, John Harrah soon lost all except one of the buildings in which he had an interest. Finally he was left with just the lease on one building on the Venice pier, which featured a not-quite-legal game based loosely on bingo.

It was called the Circle Game because players sat in a circle and rolled marbles. If your marble hit your number, you could then choose a card. If you were lucky, you would end up with a pair of kings or some other combination, as in poker, and have a chance of winning a $1.25 carton of cigarettes.

Because theoretically a skillful player could influence the movements of the ball, John Harrah was able to argue that this was a legal game of skill—not an illegal game of chance.

Sudden Change of Direction: Bill Harrah was studying mechanical engineering at U.C.L.A. when the depression began. He was able to satisfy the fairly relaxed demands of most of his professors, although much of his time was devoted to his two enthusiasms—girls and cars. But then, in 1930, he was caught cheating on a chemistry exam, and had to leave the university.

His father, who could be demanding at times, accepted the news of his son's trouble with no special concern, since his mind was on his own problems. He suggested that Bill, who was then twenty, come back to Venice and run the Circle Game for him. Bill Harrah agreed, since he saw no great future in mechanical engineering.

Soon after he went to work on the Venice pier, Bill Harrah took a close look at his father's way of running the Circle Game—and was not impressed.

First, he observed, Mr. Harrah believed in buying furnishings as cheaply as possible. When he needed something for the players to sit on while they were gambling away their nickels and dimes, he found a place to buy stools for

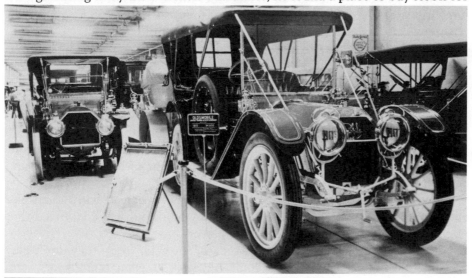

A small part of Bill Harrah's automobile collection in Reno. Harrah began collecting automobiles early, and ended up with 1,400 of them. When the IRS attempted to collect taxes on the entire collection, Harrah was outraged, his biographer, Leon Mandel, reports. "Did they think I was drivin' all 1,400?" he asked.

Benefiting from his father's mistakes, Bill Harrah learned to make players feel welcome at his tiny, crowded bingo parlor in Reno. Here, one of Harrah's employees (left) calls out the lucky numbers.

eleven dollars each. As young Bill observed, they looked like eleven-dollar stools.

Bill also realized that his father had no great respect for the people who came in to gamble—and showed it. His chief interest was in getting them in, relieving them of their small change, and getting them out as quickly as possible. This was as obvious to players as it was to Bill.

John Harrah displayed almost equal contempt for the people he hired to work at the establishment.

"Help to him were just like apples: you needed a dozen, you went and bought a dozen.

"When we opened up, he said, 'Get some help.' And when we closed up, 'Pay 'em off.' And they were like walnut pickers or somethin'."

John Harrah also used shills. He thought these hired players would convince people who were passing by that the Circle Game was very popular, and that they would join in.

Bill Harrah disagreed with this theory as he disagreed with much else about his father's way of running the Circle Game. Bill was convinced that many people quickly recognized the paid players.

"You fool the public for about two days," he said, "then they don't play with you anymore. They don't like you. They say your game is crooked."

One day he suggested to his father: "If we get rid of the shills, we're going to do fine."

"You get rid of the shills, and you're gonna lose your shirt!" his father said. "Suppose you have only two players at twenty-five cents a piece, and you're giving away a dollar and a quarter, you lose seventy-five cents a game!"

But the point he missed, Bill Harrah said, was that bingo players are actually attracted by a game with few players, since they are competing against fewer people and have a better chance of winning. He was certain that the shills actually reduced the attraction of the game for experienced bingo players.

The Five-Hundred-Dollar Gamble: After a series of arguments about the best way to run the place, John Harrah lost interest in the Circle Game and sold the entire enterprise to Bill Harrah for five hundred dollars. Young Bill's first act was to fire the shills.

"And I put in some drapes and some pretty stools, and it didn't look too bad," he recalled. The weekly profits soon doubled, then doubled again. After a while he found himself making fifty thousand dollars a year from the Circle Game, but he also began running into another problem. Games of chance had been tolerated for years along the Venice pier, but the atmosphere changed in the mid-1930s.

"You'd get a district attorney runnin' for re-election, or the chief of police, and they would arrest you on a gamblin' charge," he recalled later.

John Harrah, with his legal background, would object loudly when the Venice police came to close down the Circle Game. Harrah remembered one of these scenes:

"What are you guys—crazy?" John Harrah asked.

"We're closing all the bingo games," the policeman replied.

"This is no bingo game!" John Harrah shouted. "This is no way a bingo game! We don't use baseballs; we use marbles. We don't use bingo cards; we use playing cards. Bla bla bla bla bla bla bla blah. . . ."

For a while John Harrah was able to out-talk the police, but then a new anti-gambling crusade would begin and the Circle Game would be closed down. Both John and Bill Harrah grew weary of these encounters and the threat of fines.

"And then I came to Reno, just on a spree, with no thought of going into business," Bill Harrah remembered. This was in 1937.

At first he was as unimpressed by the town as Harold Smith had been two years earlier. With some friends he first dropped into a "real cheesy bar."

"It was terrible—I mean, bum liquor, you know, and just bum atmosphere. And we said, 'Wow, this is Reno?'"

But then they went over to the Golden Hotel, then the most luxurious establishment in Reno, and suddenly it was a different world.

"Look at that!" Harrah remembered saying to his friends. "They don't close the bars, and they don't close the games, and they leave you alone. And you know, the police were nice—everybody was so nice."

At first Harrah was afraid he had discovered Reno too late. He looked around at several prosperous little bingo parlors and thought: "I should have been here last year."

But about a month after he returned to California he received word that one of the bingo parlors he had noticed on Center Street had closed down.

"So I came up and bought it real cheap. . . ."

It was cheap for a reason: It was at Second and Center street, and that was then about three blocks away from the heart of the action. Harrah was able to keep it going just three months before going broke, but he had learned a lesson he remembered for the rest of his life: Location is everything in Reno.

He also learned a great deal more during those first months. He saw that some owners shared his father's approach to running a gambling operation: Get the people in, take whatever money they have, then hurry them on their way. Don't waste money on carpets or furnishings or the general appearance of the place. Hire help cheaply, and be ready to toss them out as soon as business began to slow down.

He saw all this, and decided to do the reverse.

Skimping on furniture and treating hired help as expendable and players as a nuisance hadn't worked well when his father was running the Circle Game, and Harrah thought it wouldn't work any better in Reno. He assumed that people who came into Harrah's would be looking for the same things that had impressed him when he went into the Golden Hotel, and that they would keep coming back if he offered them the best-run casino in the world.

"We had many cross-roaders coming in, and we could handle those pretty good," William Harrah recalled about the late 1930s. "But then we had some crooked dealers, and it was really very tough. And at times there, I wondered if we were going to make it, actually."

A Modest Beginning: At first Harrah was dealing with a few hundred dollars a day. He recalls in his oral history that he would sometimes take the day's earnings next door around 2 or 3 a.m., to one of his favorite bars, and leave the cash with the bartender for safekeeping. Occasion-

A Short History of Reno

During World War II Harrah's Club was crowded into a small area along Virginia Street in Reno, but Bill Harrah was already planning for the extraordinary growth that was to make him the operator of one of the city's most successful casinos.

ally, when the cash ran perilously low, one of Harrah's employees would go over to the same bar and borrow fifty or a hundred dollars to see the little enterprise through the night.

But that was in the early days. Soon the customers began crowding in—first by the dozens, then by the hundreds, eventually by the thousands. Harrah doubled the size of his small bingo parlor within a year. In 1942 he put in twenty slot machines, one craps table and one 21 game. As soon as World War II ended he began buying up surrounding properties in Reno (the Mint Club, the Bonanza Club, the Frontier Club, The Grand Bar and the Grand Cafe) and his first properties at Lake Tahoe (the Gateway Club, the Stateline Country Club, and the Nevada Club). His lifelong habit of using the money that was pouring in to expand the properties he owned and building grander new ones had begun.

His father watched this wild expansion of his son's properties with considerable doubt and foreboding. Mark Curtis, who later became a vice president of Harrah's, remembers that the old man would sometimes look down from a plane when approaching Reno "to see if the lights were still on at the casino."

As early as the 1930s a few casino owners began experimenting with the idea of featuring stars in their showrooms as a way of attracting gamblers. At first Harrah was skeptical about this approach, but with his first ventures at Lake Tahoe he changed his mind. He opened his South Shore Room at Tahoe with comedian Red Skelton, and featured singer Eddie Fisher during the first nights at the Headliner Room at Harrah's Reno.

Sammy Davis, Jr., later became one of his favorite performers. When Harrah offered him one million dollars for twenty-four appearances at Tahoe, Davis told reporters: "Thirty years ago I was going around doing one-nighters at ten dollars a night." Although he was trying to look cool when the new contract was announced, Davis said, "I've got sweaty palms."

Harrah pampered the stars. "He'd meet them at the Reno airport with a Rolls Royce," advertising man Tom Wilson recalled. "He built a luxurious mansion at Tahoe—finally wound up with two of 'em—where he put these actors, and all kinds of service, all kinds of recreation."

Even with the growth of his casinos, Harrah still ran into prejudices when he left Nevada. As he expanded, he decided he would like to have a major national advertising agency handle his account. He wrote to J. Walter Thompson, to Foote, Cone and Belding, and to BBD&O, indicating that he would be ready to work out arrangements with them.

"To his acute embarrassment, none of these big agencies would touch Harrah's advertising," Tom Wilson recalls. They were not about to endanger their relationship with Pacific Telephone or Pacific Gas & Electric "by taking on a gambling club."

In Reno, Harrah gained a reputation for maintaining a close watch over every detail in his casinos. One visitor to Reno once saw a tall man wearing what was obviously a very expensive, carefully tailored suit riding down an escalator, running his fingers along the underside of the moving hand rail. That was Bill Harrah, making certain that the cleaning people had taken care of dust—even where it could not be seen.

With Smith's carnival tricks and back-slapping, and Harrah's thirst for perfection, first thousands, then hundreds of thousands, then millions of visitors from Des Moines to Hong Kong began making the journey to Reno by car, bus, train or plane—changing the wild little western town forever.

Drawing a Red Line: For a while "Pappy" Smith, Bill Harrah, and the owners of a few other casinos crowded into a few blocks of downtown Reno appeared to have things all wrapped up. The city drew a red line around the small casino section, and accepted with some gratitude the license fees and the tourist dollars these glittering establishments brought in.

The pattern seemed set. Most Renoites were convinced that the handy red line would protect the rest of the city from any contamination introduced by the gamblers. The wider area outside the line would be reserved for homes, businesses, schools, the state university, movie houses, theaters, banks and churches—all the activities of small-town life.

These arrangements seemed to be widely accepted during the first twenty years of legalized gambling. But then one determined man set out to change everything.

"My job at that time was just counting the boxes," Bill Harrah said, remembering his early days in Reno. "I loved it, especially when there was a good shift, and it was fun to open those boxes and find 'em full of hundred dollar bills. . . . And a crumpled bill, even the ones, I'd straighten 'em all out. . . . Nowadays I don't think they want an owner to count the money any more because there were so many of 'em puttin' it in their pocket. . . ."

Life imitates art . . .
Reno showgirl copies
pose and costume of the
Primadonna statue.

Breaking Through the Red Line

8

By the 1950s many people in Reno felt they had succeeded in putting some boundaries around legalized gambling.

The City Council actually drew a red line around about five blocks of midtown Reno. Inside that line, new casinos could be developed, and existing casinos could be expanded. But anyone proposing the construction of a new casino *outside* the red line would have to get special permission—and there were clear signs that any such request would be speedily rejected. (Exceptions would be made for a developer who planned to build a luxury hotel with at least a hundred rooms, since the City Council felt that would help draw the kind of visitors the town needed. But there were few prospects of such projects in the 1940s and 1950s.)

The Council also permitted small shopkeepers to put in a few slot machines and install up to three blackjack tables on their premises. These little entertainment centers in cafés and grocery stores were not considered important in a city where most of the real gambling was being done in casinos.

Most of the casino owners seemed happy with the separation of their businesses from all other activities in the city. What the red line seemed to provide was a kind of licensed monopoly for those who had staked their claims soon after gambling was legalized. Latecomers would have little chance of competing for the dollars being brought into Reno by the growing flood of visitors, especially from California.

Renoites who had opposed the 1931 decision to legalize gambling were also generally pleased by the red line. At least now the casinos were clearly separated from the rest of the city, just as most brothels had been since the 1920s. (The more refined establishments were not cut off, but they were seen as appealing to a superior clientele.)

Businessmen in midtown felt that the red line would save them from higher lease or rent payments. If the line were not there, they feared that newly arriving casino developers would begin to compete for the limited business space in the center of the city and would offer the owners of downtown buildings much higher rents than the operators of small businesses could afford.

Some of those who supported the red line warned that the whole town would become "a permanent honky tonk" if other areas of Reno were opened to dozens of gambling dens. One of them said the heart of the town would become little more than "a series of slot machine arcades" if the line were dropped.

"This zone was originally established to limit gambling from the standpoint of health and morals," Reno Mayor Roy Bankofier said. "We have to keep in mind that gambling is a tolerated [but] permissive business."

Mr. Primm's Crusade: But while many defended the red line, one man was outraged by it—and set out on a passionate crusade to erase it.

His name was Ernest Primm, and he was one of the owners of a garish establishment known as the Primadonna. The Primadonna was a very visible casino, offering to visitors from small towns the eye-catching sight of five statuesque ladies who dominated a block of midtown. Not overdressed, the large-breasted ladies lighted up the night sky and gained considerable attention during the daylight hours. (Strangers occasionally tried to decide which of the ladies was Prima and which one was Donna.)

To Ernest Primm, bottled up in a narrow casino, the urge to expand his enterprise across to the forbidden west side of Virginia Street—just beyond the red line—was overwhelming. He seemed to consider the decision by the City Council to limit his growth un-American, and certainly un-Nevadan.

One legend in Reno is that Primm achieved his aim by fooling a rather dim-witted City Council. According to this story, he first obtained a permit to build a luxury restaurant just across the street from the Primadonna. Then he quietly installed a couple of slot machines, explaining to those who raised questions that these were being put there just to keep customers amused while they were waiting for a table. When no one at the City Council objected to that, he removed a couple more of his restaurant tables and brought in half a dozen more slots and a craps table. After three or four more late nights of quiet alterations, he left just enough non-gambling room for a single table for anyone who wandered into his "café" with the idea of having a hamburger.

Those who tell that story are convinced that it is true, and because owners of some Reno gambling establishments often proceed by stealth, it sounds plausible. But the printed record seems to indicate that Primm was a little more open in his campaign, although he did achieve the same objective by a series of slightly devious actions.

Primm's campaign began in 1951 when he asked for a permit to open a small bar on the west side of Virginia Street—just across the red line. This modest request was turned down by the City Council, which felt that the little town was already oversupplied with bars.

Next Primm came up with a proposal to expand his existing casino, located on the east side of Virginia Street (and inside the red line). He wanted to push it just a bit over the line, to the west.

Ernie Primm, who led to the battle to expand gambling beyond the red line, impressed Reno's visitors with the larger-than-life-size beauties who adorned his Primadonna. (The casino was later sold to Del Webb.)

The Chamber of Commerce and the Nevada Retail Merchants Association quickly realized what Primm was up to and objected strongly. Impressed by this opposition, the City Council said no.

Never a man to give in easily, Primm sued the city. A lower court ruled against him. He took the case to the state Supreme Court.

That court surprised him by issuing a sweeping decision, observing that the city had an absolute right to deny *anybody* the right to open a new casino *anywhere* within city limits.

For many developers this would have seemed the final word. Not to Primm.

Denting the Red Line: In 1954 Primm announced that he would build a new hotel on the west side of Virginia—again, just across the red line. This time the Chamber of Commerce and the Retail Merchants Association suddenly changed sides. Yes, both groups said, it would be a contribution to the city if Primm built a modern hotel "in which gambling would be incidental."

But it didn't remain "incidental" for long. Primm helped elect a new City Council that wouldn't be as difficult as the one that had delayed his plans. By 1955, he had succeeded. And the new members were not going to be difficult about it if Primm's new building happened to include a bit more gambling than first proposed.

One member of the new City Council announced openly: "My intent is to open the west side of Virginia Street between Commercial Row and Second Street" to gambling. The new Mayor, Len Harris, interrupted him to proclaim: "That's our policy."

The triumphant Primm didn't seem as grateful as the cooperative new Council might have expected. He complained that the new men, who had been in office only a few days, were going too slowly. They had told him that it would take several days to prepare the necessary formal resolution to open up the west side of that one street.

"Primm has already submitted several license applications," the *Reno Evening Gazette* reported with evident surprise. "In one he has asked to change a previous bar license to a cabaret license, permitting entertainment."

He also asked "incidentally" for: one craps table, one 21 table, one roulette game, and an additional forty-nine slot machines (to be set up near the eleven he had previously installed).

"The first move to let Reno's neon-lit gaming casinos spread west away from the Virginia downtown 'strip' for the first time in the city's history was approved yesterday by the city council. . . ."
—*Reno Evening Gazette*, May 23, 1961.

Five months later, with opposition to the expansion still strong, a *Gazette* headline proclaimed: RENO COULD DO WITHOUT GAMING, SAYS MAYOR.

A Few Modest Additions: Not long after opening his new building, Primm announced that he would like to do a little "modernization." "Most important of the changes now underway is the extension of the present building back about twenty-four feet," the *Evening Gazette* reported. "This will allow two or three more rows of slot machines toward the front, and almost double the gambling space. . . . Keno games will be expanded. . . . The restrooms will be moved toward the rear, allowing nine hundred square feet of extra gaming area. . . . Tentative plans next winter call for renovation of the entire front space to add gaming facilities. . . ."

All seemed to be going well for Mr. Primm until 1961, when he found himself facing a less cooperative City Council. When he said he thought it would be a good idea to expand his gambling enterprise a little farther to the west—far over the already badly-dented red line—the Council said no. A new Mayor, Bud Baker, went so far as to say that the city could do without gambling entirely with no great loss.

Primm would not accept this heresy. He sent out fifty workers, and in a matter of days they had collected six thousand signatures on a petition to open up the entire western area of downtown Reno to casinos. When the City Council heard that nearly two-thirds of the voters of Reno had signed Mr. Primm's petition, it caved in.

The *Evening Gazette* recorded the strange turnaround: "Some members of the Reno City Administration have changed their votes, if not their minds, on the question of extending the gambling limits to include Sierra Street."

At first, the newspaper reported, a vote to allow gambling to move farther west had divided the Council three to three, with the Mayor also voting against the change. But after the Council members heard about the petitions, the vote changed dramatically. Suddenly five members of the Council were in favor of Mr. Primm's proposal, and only one of them opposed it.

"The Council's latest action is taken, not because some of the members have changed their opinions," the paper said. "It is the only sensible thing to do when the city government finds itself facing a double-charged gun. . . . The gambler whose plans for Sierra Street expansion have been blocked at City Hall conducted a clever propaganda campaign, and it appeared that an election might give him what he wanted. . . ."

The red line was not formally erased. But it was clear that it would never again be an unbreakable barrier to a determined man who was resolved to expand casinos anywhere in the city.

The way was open now for a vast expansion of casinos in Reno, financed by wealthy investors and corporations. But before that could take place, a few fundamental problems in operating a gambling business had to be solved.

Outwitting the Crossroaders: While Ernie Primm was concentrating on breaking through the red line, other casino owners were focusing much of their attention during the 1940s, 1950s, and into the 1960s on a major dilemma around casinos: finding ways to guard against dishonest players and dishonest employees. Until the casinos could solve this and find a way to keep close track of all the money that changed hands every few minutes in a busy club, they could not attract the investors who would be ready to pour hundreds of millions of dollars into the new buildings that would occupy some of the space opened up by Primm's long campaign.

Before gambling was legalized in 1931, owners of the smoky gambling dens in Reno had worked out their own direct way of discouraging tricky gamblers (called "crossroaders") or sticky fingered employees.

Silvio Petricianni, whose father operated the old Palace Club in downtown Reno, described the method used by the toughest owners of the town's shadowy gambling dens in the 1920s—when the games were still illegal: "When they caught a crossroader, they'd take him downstairs and put his fingers in a vice and break his fingers. So that marked him, and also, he wouldn't be so adept. Crossroaders knew what the consequences would be when they went to cheat in those places."

He added: "It's no different than the barbaric systems used by Orientals when they wanted to question somebody and they'd put bamboo shoots under their fingernails. I mean . . . this wasn't so much a method of torture as a method of punishment, because, you know, back then you couldn't afford to have somebody cheat you. In those days, if they cheated you out of fifty dollars or a hundred dollars, that was a big score. . . ."

Viewed With Suspicion: With the growth of legalized gambling, owners realized that the traditional methods of enforcing honesty required some refining. They devised a surveillance system that workers in most businesses would have found intolerable. It was based on absolute distrust of many of the players and of every employee who handled money.

The deep suspicions about their customers might seem unwarranted. But many people who have worked in casinos for years are convinced that players

are capable of trying almost any way to beat a casino, since those players also assume that the house has an overwhelming, unfair advantage in every game.

"It's almost impossible for people to believe that the greatest worry in a gaming operation is the dishonesty of the customer," said Leslie Kofoed, who worked closely with the Smiths at Harolds Club.

"We found over the years that they'll try any kind of gimmick to beat the house. The feeling seems to be . . . that any tactics are fair, and every operator is fair game."

The simplest form of cheating was the use of foreign coins or slugs in slot machines. But then, Kofoed said, "The state legislature saw fit to outlaw the use of foreign coins or slugs in the machine, not because it wanted to protect the operator at all, but because the slots were on a gross tax. And every time a customer put in a coin of no value, the state of Nevada and the gaming commission were losing money."

More ambitious crossroaders would glue a fine wire to a coin, and use that to pull a coin back out of the slot after a play, before it had disappeared into the machine. In this way they could play the same nickel or dime or quarter for an hour, if no one in the casino observed them closely. This trick became so widely used that some machines were equipped with a scissoring device that would reach out and cut the wire or string.

Crossroaders' Tricks: A few players developed elaborate electronic devices through which they could control loaded dice. Others worked out a contraption which could be concealed under a player's jacket and activated by a shrug of the shoulder. It would feed the desired card into the palm of the gambler's hand.

Some experimented for a while with an elaborate combination: cards marked with a special, generally invisible ink that could only be seen by a player who was wearing a particular type of contact lens. There was one major problem with this: the lenses used by these crossroaders were an unusual color and could be detected quickly by a dealer who had been trained to watch for them.

In the early days, when the drop boxes (built to hold the dollars players paid to dealers when buying chips at the tables) were made of wood, one crossroader would distract the dealer while another would crawl under the table and rifle the box—"just cleaning all the currency out of it," Leslie Kofoed recalled.

All of these were small-time operations, and caused relatively small losses. There have been far more ambitious schemes—especially those carried out from the inside.

One gang set up its own counting room in a Reno casino and siphoned off nearly two million dollars by selling players hundreds of thousands of packets of coins that were one or two coins short. (The originators of this scam had observed that very, very few players bother to check to be sure they are actually getting two dollars' worth of nickels or ten dollars' worth of quarters when they are caught up in the excitement of casino play.)

In Las Vegas, a casino thought it had discovered a sure way to cut its losses from crossroaders. In his oral history, Bill Harrah commented on the results:

> Jay VanderMark is the fellow that was put in charge of the slot machines at the Stardust. He's probably one of the best slot machine thieves in the whole United States, and they figured if they put him in charge of the slots they'd be protected. Jay was quite a character. Old, talked with a drawl, had a hearing aid . . . and he'd give you this wide-eyed innocent look. . . .

Silvio Petricianni, whose father owned one of the earliest Reno casinos, remembers the method operators worked out to deal with players who tried to stop payment on the checks they had given to settle their gambling debts. "On Monday, I would leave Reno about four o'clock in the morning, drive down to Sacramento or San Francisco or wherever it was and be the first in line at the bank to cash their checks. And the gamblers would come by next week or so and just raise seven kinds of hell with me, saying, 'How could you do this to me?' And I would say, 'Because you were going to do it to me.'"

A Short History of Reno

Wide-eyed, innocent looking Jay did manage to spot some crossroaders at the Stardust. And then, one day, just when the casino felt it had solved its problems with cheaters, Jay disappeared—with four million dollars of the casino's cash.

Disappearing Cash: Cheating by both players and employees was so common in Harolds Club, Bill Harrah recalled, that "Pappy" Smith once said to him, "We have to win the money twice."

While the club was winning a thousand dollars at the table, Smith explained, roughly an equal amount would be disappearing into the pockets of cheating players or crooked employees. So with that percentage lost, it was necessary for the club to win two thousand dollars to end up the day one thousand dollars ahead.

Later, when Harrah built his place at Lake Tahoe, he would occasionally show friends through his huge casino there. On the Fourth of July, soon after the opening, when thousands of people were crowded onto the gambling floors, one of his friends asked him: "How do you handle all this? How can you keep from getting robbed blind?"

"And the answer is, no way you could do it," Harrah told him. "You just couldn't open it up and hire a bunch of people and not get robbed."

But as time went on, he said, he chose a few men he had complete trust in and gave them the job of watching over the whole place for him. "Pretty soon, everybody's honest but two or three people," he said.

The Unblinking Eye: Some of the early casinos occupied old structures that had been haphazardly reconstructed to serve as gambling halls. In adapting them, the owners ordered the construction of an intricate network of catwalks above the ceilings of the gambling floors.

Concealed from both players and employees by one-way mirrors, these catwalks were patrolled by unseen overseers—the men who became known as "The Eye in the Sky."

The Eye—usually an experienced, trusted former dealer or pit boss—made his way along a rough boardwalk, through clusters of air ducts and dust-covered water pipes or wires. Moving with the dexterity of a cat, he would focus his attention on the casino floor, looking for any suspicious movement by a player, a dealer, a cashier, those who watched over the paper money (in the soft count room), or those who worked in the rooms where coins were counted and packaged.

If he saw anything that might indicate dishonest behavior, he quickly communicated his observations to a pit boss or a security chief.

What the owner wanted to achieve by hiring the hidden Eye was uncertainty. And he did. Any casino employee who was thinking of slipping a ten-dollar bill or a couple of chips inside the waistband of his pants was likely to hesitate and think again if he felt there was somebody up there beyond that mirror, watching.

The chief security problem in a casino arises from the constant flow of hundreds of thousands of dollars from hand to hand during every shift. (Over a busy weekend, employees in a big casino might handle four or five million dollars.) Players cash checks, buy chips, get change for the slots, tip dealers and the girls who bring them free drinks, and pay for meals ranging from hotdogs to broiled salmon. Without adequate safeguards, many thousands of dollars a day could be siphoned off, and the bankruptcy of a few casinos over the years has been blamed on the owner's failure to keep close watch over the way the money was handled.

To make cheating by employees more difficult, the owners required many employees to wear uniforms with no pockets, and to prove their honesty by rubbing their hands together briskly after each transaction, then holding their open palms up toward the ceiling, to prove to the Eye that they hadn't concealed either cash or chips. (One long-time casino employee said he found himself raising his open palms upward after paying for groceries in a Safeway supermarket.)

About successful slot machine cheaters, Silvio Petricianni said, "People came in with holes in their jeans, and they went out driving Cadillacs. . . ."

Watching Over the Owners: While the owners were concerned about the honesty of their employees, the state of Nevada was preoccupied with the possibility that some of the millions flowing into the casinos might pass into the pockets of the owners without a percentage being turned over to the state in taxes.

Everyone knew that some of the owners had been a little casual about handling money during the early days of legalized gambling—in the 1930s and 1940s. The idea of dipping into the free-flowing cash to buy drinks all around, or give a thousand-dollar bonus to a popular entertainer, or to help out a friend who had a bad day at the tables seemed harmless. But as the profits from gambling grew (from a few hundred thousands to many millions), the state began watching over the casino operators with the same unblinking eye that the owners had focused on their employees.

The widespread use of the computer made casino accounting—and the quick detection of any fiddling with the cash—much easier.

Bill Harrah was one of the first to make full use of the computers (although he often said he had no idea how they worked). He found that with these mysterious machines he could discover exactly how much profit he was making on every slot machine during every shift. He could learn the exact number of dollars played at every 21 table, how much cash each of the restaurants was generating, and the daily occupancy rate in his huge and profitable hotels. He could also spot immediately any trouble spot in the house.

The Word Spreads: Most of the Reno casinos were owned by individuals and families during the early years, but in the 1950s the word began to get around about just how much men like Bill Harrah and the Smiths were making from their relatively small casinos. This inevitably attracted the attention of investors who had previously shied away from gambling enterprises. Major corporations and wealthy businessmen were suddenly ready to risk hundreds of millions on buying and building casinos. Banks, which for decades had refused to lend money to casino owners, were suddenly willing to talk about major loans. A great boom in building was about to start.

The Mysterious Mr. Hughes: A major figure in this new development was the reclusive billionaire Howard Hughes. There were reports that he had around five hundred million in cash as a result of his sale of TWA, and suddenly he began buying Nevada casinos. Hughes spent nearly a quarter of a billion dollars on six hotel casinos in four years—between 1966 and 1970. But five of these were in Las Vegas, and only one—Harolds Club, now aged, neglected, and a little shabby—was located in Reno.

Hughes kept sending indirect messages to Bill Harrah from his darkened hotel room in Las Vegas, where he lived unseen by people who ran his empire.

Robert Maheu, Hughes's representative, kept trying to set up a meeting between Harrah and Hughes, but that never worked out. One day Maheu asked Harrah directly, "Do you wanna sell?"

"No," Harrah said. But then he added: "I don't believe saying something isn't for sale. Anything's for sale. If you want to pay me double what it's worth, I'll consider it." And he emphasized: "It's no bargains around here."

Maheu continued to dicker with Harrah. "He'd come out to my house at two in the morning a lot, and he would pretend to call Hughes. I think really he *was* calling him. And he'd say, 'Harrah says this,' and 'Harrah says that.' And so on and so on.

"Hughes really liked to buy things for nothin'. Nothin' wrong with that—I like to do that too." But an acceptable offer never came, and Harrah was still the chief owner of his casinos at the time of his death.

The fact that Hughes had risked a sizeable part of his wealth on casinos influenced other major investors, including several corporations. Suddenly the

The eccentric multimillion-aire Howard Hughes often expressed his interest in Bill Harrah's casinos through a series of after-midnight calls from his Las Vegas hide-away, but he never offered enough to tempt Harrah. Here Hughes is shown during the days when he was still squiring a series of stars and starlets, before he went into isolation, occupy-ing complete hotel floors, concealed from public view behind drawn curtains.

A Short History of Reno

Del Webb Corporation, Hilton Hotels, MGM, Ramada Inns and Holiday Inns all began exploring the possibility of buying existing casinos or building new ones.

Before the 1970s boom, Reno had only two major hotel-casinos. Then, in one quick burst, new ones began opening, one after another: the huge MGM Grand, the Sahara-Reno, Circus Circus, the Comstock, the Money Tree, the Onslow, and the Colonial Inn. Half a dozen others began expanding, including Harrah's.

The most spectacular of the new casinos was built by the rarely seen president of MGM, Kirk Kerkorian.

Kerkorian had made millions from the MGM Grand in Las Vegas and decided to build on an even grander scale in Reno. He bought some land near the Paiute tribal reservation out near the Reno airport, and constructed a vast Mayan-style structure at a cost of $131,000,000. It was then the largest casino in the world, with just over a thousand rooms, two thousand slot machines, and something over three thousand employees.

It had taken a long time. But in the 1970s, just a little over a century after Myron Lake built Lake House on the banks of the Truckee, the Biggest Little City in the World seemed ready to live up to its slogan. A new age seemed about to begin.

Looking back at his early days in Reno, Bill Harrah recalled: "Many of those years I was very insecure. I kept up a pretty good front, you know. I looked good, and my clothes were good, and my car was good, but inside I was really scared. I didn't really think I 'had it' and anyone that was successful, I admired and wondered how they did it. And I didn't think, really, that I would ever get anywhere. And when I did have some success, it was so gratifying because it was such a surprise. *Me!* You know, of all people. I really felt real—what's the word—incapable, really— of doing anything. You know, sure, I could park cars or somethin', but as far as runnin' a business— it's funny."

Biggest Little City

9

All night long, night after night, downtown Reno is wide awake with gamblers, strollers and insomniacs. Colored lights glitter and flash on Virginia Street, spelling out the names of casinos: Harrah's, Harolds, Nevada Club, Cal-Neva and The Virginian on one side of the street. Fitzgerald's, Horseshoe Club, El Dorado, Silver Legacy, Circus Circus and the tiny Nugget on the opposite side. A block away on Sierra Street, lights of the Flamingo Hilton cast a pink glow on the sidewalk; Dixieland jazz blares from the Riverboat; the Comstock beckons down Second Street.

Centerpiece for all this glitter—like a decoration on top of an ornate wedding cake—is the Reno Arch, background for a million tourist snapshots. Spanning Virginia Street between the railroad and Commercial Row, the arch proclaims Reno

THE BIGGEST LITTLE CITY IN THE WORLD.

Bright red neon tubing—800 feet of it—forms the four letters of the city's name. Beneath the big neon "RENO," the famous slogan, wider than the steet, is illuminated by sixteen hundred light bulbs.

The current arch is the latest in a series of Reno arches, going back to the turn of the century. Tracking down the origins of the city's arches, Nevada historian Phillip I. Earl discovered photographs of an arch built in 1899.

"So far as we know," he wrote in the *Reno Gazette-Journal*, "the first arch to grace Virginia Street was put up on the old iron bridge across the Truckee River in November, 1899, as part of the community's welcome for Troop A, First Nevada Volunteer Cavalry, returning from duty in the Philippines during

Opposite page
Reno's nightime skyline.

the Spanish-American War." That arch carried the simple message, "Welcome Home."

While searching for details about early arches, Earl also found references to Reno's durable slogan.

"At the time of the famed Johnson-Jeffries heavyweight championship fight, July 4, 1910," Earl wrote, "a group of outside journalists suggested that Reno officials adopt the slogan, 'Biggest Little City in the World,' but it did not get into general circulation."

Earl also found an article about "Reno: Biggest Little City on the Map," published in 1912 by the Reno Commercial Club, and a reference to a "Biggest Little City" banner carried by a Reno attorney in a 1914 parade staged by the national Grand Lodge of Moose in Chicago. Still, the slogan didn't seem to catch on.

Meanwhile, the city continued to erect arches to celebrate big events. In the fall of 1914, visitors passing through Reno on their way to the Panama-Pacific Exposition in San Francisco were greeted by an arch across Virginia Street. The Nevada Historical Society has no record of a slogan—if there was one—on that early arch.

Seven decades later, Andrew Ginocchio, a young Reno blacksmith in 1914, remembered his own part in erecting the Panama-Pacific arch:

"It was a hot summer day," the president of Reno Iron Works recalled in a 1987 oral history, "when two men from Nevada Transfer and three men from Armstrong Manufacturing Co., started at 8 a.m. to assemble and erect the arch. I was the third man, a helper. . . . My job was to drill holes in the concrete. The city engineer had designed the foundation."

Later a consultant on the building of the San Francisco Bay Bridge and a trainer of welders during World War II, Ginocchio gained worldwide recognition for his metal-working skills. Still, he held vivid memories of the day he worked on the Reno arch.

"It was built in San Francisco," he explained. "It arrived by rail in three sections—two pillars and the cross section. It was unloaded at the Southern Pacific Depot in Reno . . . and brought to the site on Virginia Street."

The men worked until noon, then adjourned to Becker's Saloon on Commercial Row, a favorite hangout where they could buy a beer and lunch for 15 cents. Until his death in 1988, the 94-year-old Ginocchio still talked about that day in 1914.

Six years later, in June 1920, the Reno Roundup Association put up a new arch, strung with electric lights, to advertise its three-day rodeo and Wild

Reno's flamboyant Mayor E. E. Roberts opened the 1927 Transcontinental Highway Exposition, jointly sponsored by California and Nevada, in Idlewild Park. The state of California donated a building—still called the California Building and still used in the 1990s for recreational programs and public events.

A Short History of Reno

West Show. "Reno Welcomes You" was the message on the arch, facing the railroad tracks where train travelers couldn't miss it.

The completion of the Lincoln and Victory Highways through Reno in the summer of 1927 called for a celebration. The city planned to welcome more visitors than ever. What could be more appropriate—more typically RENO—than a new arch with a message spelled out in lights?

So the new arch was built and dedicated on October 23, 1926. Glittering letters advertised the "Reno Transcontinental Highway Exposition, June 25—August 1." For ten months, anticipating the Exposition, lights on the arch were turned on every night. When the celebration ended, the advertising came down—but the arch remained.

The new highway, U.S. Route 40, removed some of the dread of "The Great American Desert" felt by many travelers and vacationers. For the first time, in 1927, Reno became easily accessible.

Search for a Slogan: Without its lit-up message, the arch looked a little bare. So the Reno City Council started looking around for a permanent slogan. In the summer of 1928 the council announced a contest, offering a prize of a hundred dollars to the creator of the best Reno motto. Judges

"Miss Press Photographer" and friends under the Reno arch c. 1959.

wanted something short—to fit on the space vacated by the Highway Exposition ad—but it had to express, somehow, the flavor of the whole city. Entries were varied:

> Reno: Nevada's Silver Lily
> Reno: Where Life's Worth Living
> Reno: A City Unrestrained In Its Enjoyment of Natural Rights
> Reno: Paradise of the West
> Reno: A City of Sunshine with Warm Welcomes for All

One opportunist suggested, "Reno: If You Are In A Rush, We Will Get You A Divorce in Three Months." These suggestions—and hundreds more—were rejected. Too long, too trite, too flowery. But G. A. Burns of Sacramento captured the prize with his slogan, "Reno: The Biggest Little City in the World."

Some council members said the slogan was "by no means original," but judges agreed they hadn't seen anything else that described the city so efficiently.

Reno boosters got their wish and the slogan went up in lights. A crowd gathered under the arch on June 25, 1929, and Governor Fred Balzar pulled a ceremonial switch, declaring Reno "The Biggest Little City in the World."

Around the globe, Reno's slogan caught the public fancy. Everybody who read the tabloids knew about the unique little frontier town in the Wild, Wild West where celebrities went to gamble and get divorced. Front page photos of these celebrities showed the famous Reno arch as a backdrop.

When the depression hit Reno in the early 1930s, city accountants started counting pennies. Keeping the arch lit up every night was costing too much, they said. Bulbs kept burning out and having to be replaced. Electricity for the sign was costing at least thirty dollars a month, a substantial sum in those lean years. So, on November 4, 1932, the sign was turned off.

It stayed dark for five months while local business owners argued that the advertising value of the sign was far more than the cost of keeping it lit. Finally, these business people raised the money to support the sign. Triumphantly, they turned it on again, April 17, 1933.

But you can't please everybody. By this time, Reno was famous as the only place in the United States where gambling was legal and divorce was quick and simple. Wealthy visitors poured in from everywhere. Such a sophisticated town, some people argued, didn't really need a corn-ball slogan at all. They voted to remove the "Biggest Little City" lights and to give the whole arch a brand new look, suitable for a very modern resort.

Neon was the bright new advertising medium of the thirties. What Reno needed, the City Council decided, was a tasteful neon arch. They asked for bids and accepted a simple design that would spell "RENO" in green neon—without any distracting slogans.

When the sign went up, objections were loud enough to be heard in Carson City. It seemed that nobody liked the green neon—not even those who thought Reno had outgrown its slogan. Loudest protests came from those who insisted that Reno WAS the biggest little city in the world. Why not proclaim it?

By June 12, 1935, a new neon sign was telling visitors they had arrived in the "Biggest Little City." That arch became a permanent fixture on Virginia Street for almost thirty years.

It began to show its age in the revolutionary sixties. The neon letters sometimes flickered and the whole arch looked a little rusty around the edges. Roy Powers, then a publicist for Harolds Club, led a 1963 campaign to raise one hundred thousand dollars for a new arch. When it was completed, the city staged a New Year's Eve party to light up the arch and usher in 1964.

Less than twenty years later, the city was talking about erecting another arch—not to replace the downtown structure but to supplement it. This one was designed to span Interstate Highway 80 at the downtown Reno exit, catching the attention of anyone traveling that way to California.

Richard Moreno's report in the *Reno Gazette-Journal*, October 28, 1983, described the proposed arch as "a lightly-colored rainbow of acrylic bands attached to an outer edge of chain-link fencing."

The Federal Highway Administration didn't like that idea at all. In a letter, the FHA rejected the plan, saying freeway overpasses "should be simple and dignified, devoid of any tendency toward flamboyant advertising, and in general conformance with other freeway signing."

The letter didn't discourage City Manager Chris Cherches. In October 1983 he told reporters, "I've had to ask our Congressional delegation to intercede." He was still optimistic about the arch.

The highway arch was doomed, but Reno's City Council had more ambitious plans to think about. Eight months earlier, Cherches had announced a multi-million dollar downtown redevelopment plan.

New in 1964, this Reno arch welcomed visitors to the Biggest Little City for more than 20 years.

Big Plans for RENOvation: Designs called for waterfalls and walkways along the Truckee River, trees and shrubs along Virginia Street, a big new shopping mall and restaurant complex, and a civic square and fountain in front of the Pioneer Auditorium.

The plan wasn't brand new. As early as 1968, a group of business and political leaders calling themselves "RENOvation, Inc." had commissioned a master plan for downtown Reno.

That plan, too, was ambitious. It called for the demolition of several city blocks, to be replaced by an indoor shopping mall. Designs included fountains and artificial trees along Virginia Street and an inflated rubber dam to create a marina in the Truckee River.

RENOvation turned out to be too expensive, so the plan was dropped. Then, in 1983, many of the same ideas were revived. Early that year, the Reno *Gazette* reported that City Manager Chris Cherches felt confident that by 1987 or 1988 "Reno will have its downtown mall, waterfalls, walkways and sidewalk cafes along the river."

By November, the 1983 plan had been shelved along with earlier proposals. "Another nice idea that never materialized," the *Gazette* commented.

Downtown Reno was still glittery, but signs of decay marred the city's good-time image. The elegant old Mapes, a landmark since 1948, had been boarded up. The Mapes-owned Money Tree had gone broke, just two years after a big expansion in 1978.

The Gold Dust was closed and the almost-new Onslow was about to follow it into oblivion. Del Webb's Primadonna was long gone. His extravagant Sahara had become the Reno Hilton, no longer a showcase for Broadway revivals like My *Fair Lady* and *Hello, Dolly!* Even the grande dame of Reno hotel-casinos, the Riverside, closed down its games in 1986, remaining a hotel for one more year.

But the city's innovators refused to give up. Wincing at the sight of so many boarded-up casinos, business leaders continued to talk about a new look for downtown Reno and a broader base for the city's economy. Obviously, the gambling boom wasn't going to last forever.

Early in 1987, determined to do something constructive, these civic-minded men and women formed the Biggest Little City Committee. Chairman Mark Curtis, retired vice president for advertising and public relations at Harrah's, called on everybody who cared about the city to help rescue downtown Reno. Beyond downtown, the group would set goals for improving the whole community.

At a public meeting in the Peppermill Hotel-Casino Convention Center on February 4, 1987, more than three hundred people came to offer ideas.

They drew up a list of ambitious goals reaching far beyond tourist attractions and economic development.

The Other Reno: After all, there were people who lived in Reno all their lives without gambling or getting divorced. A typical lifetime resident might have been born at St. Mary's Hospital, played in Wingfield and Idlewild Parks, gone to school at Billinghurst and Reno High, earned a degree from the University of Nevada and married in the First Methodist Church.

There were teachers who acted in Reno Little Theater productions, doctors who supported the Reno Philharmonic and Chamber Orchestras, car salesmen who sang in the chorus with the Nevada Opera. Some people worked in supermarkets, offices and shopping malls and attended classes at Truckee Meadows Community College in their spare time. What kind of town did they want?

The Biggest Little City Committee set to work. Within six months they had achieved very visible results. Most visible was a brand new Reno arch. Newsman Warren Lerude, former editor and publisher of Reno newspapers and a founding member of the Biggest Little City Committee, described the dedication ceremony:

"On August 4, 1987, twenty thousand people gathered on Virginia Street. The crowd spread for blocks north and south of the new arch. Dramatically, casino lights were turned off and a switch was thrown. Reno's new arch announced its heritage and future simultaneously in a burst of light and color. The crowd roared."

The new arch wasn't the only project begun by the Biggest Little City Committee that year, but it was one of the first. At the February meeting, Mark Curtis had asked the crowd to think about Reno's image—the way the city was seen by the rest of the world.

"We are what we are," he said, "but we are not dull. We are colorful, flamboyant, somewhat shocking, with a knack for generating a lot of headlines. There is a mystique. Perhaps we're even thought of as a little sinful. But the perception doesn't drive people away."

Critics of the "Biggest Little City" slogan were shouted down once more. When the new arch was unveiled, the slogan blazed across Virginia Street, brighter than ever. It's still the city's best known symbol.

"In a boastful but friendly way," said Curtis, "the slogan says we're not shy

During local celebrations—like the annual Reno Rodeo and Hot August Nights—the Reno arch is the centerpiece for parades and street fairs. Once a year, the Reno Philharmonic attracts crowds to an outdoor concert under the arch. Listeners bring folding chairs or stand on sidewalks beneath bright marquees proclaiming celebrity entertainment, JUMBO JACKPOTS, and BREAKFASTS $1.49.

Still the city's best-known symbol, the latest Reno arch glitters with 1,600 light bulbs under the red neon name.

about our reputation. We're still a frontier in many ways. Many of us were attracted to Reno because it was unpretentious and didn't condone hypocrisy. . . . The arch represents much more than a symbol of tourism. It really does say a lot about the vitality of the city—past, present and future."

Curtis recalls occasional efforts to dump the slogan. "It's because they think it's 'beneath' the city—or the city has outgrown it," he explained. He reminds these critics that other cities have well-known slogans. New York is "The Big Apple." Chicago is "The Windy City" and Philadelphia is "The City of Brotherly Love." But none of these, says Curtis, "has as much currency as 'The Biggest Little City.'"

By 1989 the Biggest Little City Committee was working with the Reno Redevelopment Agency to build—at last—the long-promised downtown plaza on the Truckee River. In the *Reno Gazette-Journal*, May 11, 1989, reporter Susan Voyles wrote: "The plaza is intended to be a 'people' place, where art shows can be held in the pavilion and vendors with carts will sell goodies."

It was to be built on the riverbank beside the then-closed Hotel Riverside, not far from the spot where Myron Lake sold drinks to early frontiersmen in the 1860s. The new plaza would be called the Truckee River Fountain Walk.

Downtown Facelift: When it opened in the summer of 1991, the new riverside plaza had been renamed to honor a casino pioneer. The Raymond I. Smith Truckee River Walk beckoned visitors to a weekend celebration with live entertainment, balloons and food carts. Strollers discovered a gallery of metal sculptures along the water's edge.

During the next few years, workers in downtown offices and casinos made the River Walk a favorite spot for brown-bag lunches and outdoor reading beside the recycled waterfall. Out-of-town visitors stopped to rest on benches in the gazebos.

Reno's facelift had begun, but the innovators weren't through. With the spread of legalized gambling to other states, local economists were advising Reno planners to find new ways to attract tourists.

"Probably, the best that we can hope for," said William R. Eadington, professor of economics at the University of Nevada, Reno, "is to develop the continuing loyalty of visitors who will come here not just for gambling. The real challenge is when people have the choice of going to casinos very close to where they live. What will motivate them to come to Reno? . . . That motivation doesn't have to be linked to casinos anymore—and that is quite a change."

In the early 1990s, inventive planners announced big ideas for renovating downtown Reno. There was talk of enclosing several city blocks under a dome, creating a downtown Disneyland of family entertainment with Hollywood special effects. The Reno City Council considered this idea, along with proposals for an aquarium, a downtown shopping mall, a bowling center, a special events plaza and variations on earlier scenarios proposed over the years.

Each new proposal made headlines, then seemed forgotten—until bulldozers suddenly appeared (overnight, it seemed) to clear the way for ambitious developments.

By the mid-nineties, Reno had its Silver Legacy Resort Casino, a 1,720-room joint project uniting the Circus Circus and Eldorado casinos. The huge National Bowling Stadium opened in 1995, in time to welcome nearly

"Celebrate the River" was the slogan when the six-million-dollar Raymond I. Smith Truckee River Walk was opened to strollers in downtown Reno in 1991. Almost a quarter of a century after it was first proposed, the riverside oasis was still controversial. Some critics didn't like the mauve color scheme, others objected to the "trendy" design. What would Reno's founder, Myron Lake, have said about the new look at "Lake's Crossing"? His great-great grandson, interior designer Bruce Goff, approved the walk. "It invites you to explore its sculptures and fountains," he said.

Reno's National Bowling Stadium opened in 1995, attracting bowlers from around the world.

100,000 members of the American Bowling Congress during the ABC's 100th anniversary celebration.

Downtown Reno remained the center of a 24-hour city, but some of the biggest casinos were far removed from the old red-line neighborhood. The Peppermill on South Virginia Street more than doubled its hotel space and added convention facilities long before the Clarion, conveniently located close to the Reno-Sparks Convention Center, added a new tower in 1995.

For a dozen years or more, the mammoth casino that began as the MGM, then became Bally's and later the Reno Hilton, siphoned off busloads of downtown gamblers. Future plans include a "Big West" theme resort, beginning with the Grand Canyon Buffet. Near the airport, this Hilton now attracts families as well as gamblers.

Boomtown, near Verdi, a favorite with truck drivers and highway travelers, expanded its family fun attractions with virtual reality rides and games for children.

Looking beyond the glitter of casinos, Reno city planners continued to watch for ways to preserve the city's unique reputation, considering the needs of permanent residents as well as visitors.

A University of Nevada study, a few years ago, told city planners that most Renoites don't think of the gaming industry as the most important reason for living here. "Cultural attractions, recreational opportunities, and the small-town atmosphere" were listed as major reasons for liking the town.

This doesn't mean that Reno residents ignore the casinos. Ask any Reno businessman where he had lunch yesterday and he'll mention a casino restaurant, nine times out of ten. Families flock to these restaurants for birthday celebrations—or just for a night out. Convention rooms at the glitter palaces provide meeting space for charity fund-raisers, Rotary club meetings, and wedding receptions. Casinos are simply taken for granted in Reno, like movie theaters and clubhouses in other towns.

People who live in Reno also take for granted the "big name" entertainers who perform in casino showrooms, but locals often join tourists to see a show. When the annual Reno Rodeo comes to town, the Livestock Center is filled with an indistinguishable mix of visitors and hometown folks. When the Reno Philharmonic plays at San Rafael Park to launch the Great Reno Balloon Race in September, the crowd assembles from everywhere, including houses down the street.

"Come for the action . . . come for the stars . . . come for the fun in the sun!" shouts a Reno Tahoe Tourist Guide.

Millions of visitors, whatever they come for, keep on coming back.

A coyote, cast in bronze, is one of the menagerie of sculptures created for the Raymond I. Smith Truckee River Walk by California artist John Battenberg.

More About Reno...

A Selected Bibliography

Clark, Walter Van Tilburg, *City of Trembling Leaves*, Random House, New York, 1945. A novel about growing up in Reno before World War II.

De Quille, Dan (William Wright), *The Big Bonanza*, Alfred Knopf, New York, 1967. Irreverent account of the Comstock silver boom, by Mark Twain's pal.

Dondero, Don (with Jean Stoess), *Dateline: Reno*, photographs by Dondero, Reno, 1991. Showgirls, celebrities and politicos, with reminiscences.

Earl, Phillip I., *This Was Nevada*, Nevada Historical Society, Reno, 1986. Collection of historical sketches and newspaper columns.

Elliott, Russell R., *History of Nevada*, University of Nebraska Press, Lincoln, second edition, 1987. Scholarly chronological details and maps.

Fey, Marshall, *Slot Machines: A Pictorial History of the First 100 Years*, Reno, 1989. Gallery of color photos of the old one-armed bandits.

Highton, Jake, *Nevada Newspaper Days*, Heritage West, Stockton, 1990. Veteran newsman's history of journalism and journalists in the Silver State.

Hulse, James W., *Forty Years in the Wilderness*, University of Nevada Press, Reno, 1986. Historian's candid impressions of Nevada 1940–1980.

Hulse, James W., *The Nevada Adventure*, University of Nevada Press, Reno, 1965 and 1981. Earlier history and personal reminiscences.

Laxalt, Robert, *Nevada: A History*, W. W. Norton, New York, 1977 and University of Nevada Press, 1991. Concise and perceptive history written for "The States and the Nation," a national series.

Laxalt, Robert, *Sweet Promised Land*, Harper, New York, 1957 and University of Nevada Press, 1986. Nevada classic about a Basque sheepherder who returns to the old country and discovers he has become an American.

Melton, Rollan, *Nevadans*, University of Nevada Press, Reno, 1988. Collection of newspaper columns by former editor and publisher of the *Reno-Gazette Journal*.

Nielson, Norm, *Tales of Nevada*, Volumes 1 and 2, Reno, 1989 and 1990. Lively sketches, from the author's radio broadcasts.

Nielson, Norm, *Reno: The Past Revisited*, Reno Chamber of Commerce, 1988. Concise history, with photographs.

Paher, Stanley, *Nevada: An Annotated Bibliography*, Nevada Publications, Las Vegas, 1980. Five hundred pages of Nevada references, including periodicals.

Paher, Stanley (Ed.), *Nevada Towns and Tales*, Nevada Publications, Las Vegas, 1981. Collection of historical accounts and recollections by Nevadans.

Rowley, William, *Reno: Hub of Washoe County*, Reno, 1984. Good color art and old photographs.

Shepperson, Wilbur (Ed.), *East of Eden, West of Zion*, University of Nevada Press, Reno, 1989. Essays by twelve prominent Nevada authors.

Townley, John Mark, *Reno: Tough Little Town on the Truckee*, Reno, 1983. Carefully detailed history.

ABOUT THE AUTHORS

Together and separately, Barbara and Myrick Land are the authors of fifteen books. They moved to Reno when he joined the journalism faculty at the University of Nevada after a magazine editing career in New York at *World Week, This Week* and *LOOK*. She became a reporter and feature writer for the *Reno Gazette-Journal*, continuing a newspaper career that included the *New York Times*.

The Lands met as students at the Columbia University Graduate School of Journalism where both won Pulitzer Travel Scholarships. Since then, they have lived and worked in Australia, Germany and England as well as the United States. After a dozen years in Reno, they call Nevada home.

Index

American Mercury 52
An Apartment for Peggy 65
Andy Hardy's Blonde Trouble 65
Atwood, Melville 25

Baker, Bud 105
Balloon Races 27, 125
Bally's 55, 124
Balzar, Fred 43, 59, 118
Bank Club 38, 40
Bankofier, Roy 102
Barbara Worth, Nevada 64
Bartlett, George A. 46
Baruch, Bernard 77
Battenberg, John 125
Bear River 10
Beebe, Lucius 81
Belasco, David 63
Bell, Rex 60
Berry, William B. 50–51
Big Bonanza 72, 75
Big Four 75
Biggest Little City Committee 120–123
Biltz, Norman 59–61
Black Rock Desert 8
Blasdel, H. G. 33
Boles, Lloyd 52
Boothe, Clare 45, 46
Brokaw, George 46
Buchanan, James 11
Bucke, Richard 22
Buenaventura River 8
Bull Pen 40
Burns, G. A. 118
Butler, Jim 35

California Building 116
Caples, Robert 7
Carson City 12, 19, 30, 76, 77
Carson Valley 13, 21
Celebrity marriages 54
Central Pacific Railroad 13–15, 17, 30, 75
Chaplin, Charlie 52
Cherches, Chris 119, 120
Chinatown 28–29
Chinese 14, 28
Circle Game 92–96
City Council 101–105, 117, 119, 123
Civil War 11, 14, 19, 30
Clemens, Orion 19
Clemens, Samuel 19–20, 27. *Also see* Mark Twain
Comstock Company 24
Comstock, Henry 22–24, 26
Comstock Lode 11–16, 20–22, 24, 26–27, 30–31, 47, 61–63, 72, 74
Cooper, Gary 64
Cord, E. L. 60
Corey, William Ellis and Laura 48
"The Cottage" 42
Crocker, Charles 13, 15, 17
Crossroaders 106–109
Curler, Ben 47
Curtis, Lincoln 55
Curtis, Mark 120–122

Daggett, Rollin 20
Daily Alta 61
Daily Nevada State Journal 35
Davis, Sammy, Jr. 68–69, 98
DeCicco, Pat 50
De Quille, Dan 20, 22, 24, 61
Dillinger, John 39
Divorce laws 46–47, 50–51, 53, 57
Dondero, Don 67, 83, 88

Donner, George 9
Donner, Jake 9
Donner Lake 9
Donner Party 9–10
Donner Pass 9
Doten, Alf 12, 36
Dude ranches 51–52, 57
"The Duke of Nevada" 59
Dyer's 63

El Rancho Vegas Hotel 54
"End of the Line" 17
Entertainment, live 67–68
"Eye in the Sky" 107, 109–110

Fair, James G. 75–76
Fairbanks, Douglas 49
Filmmaking 63–67
Finney, James 23–24, 26
Fleischmann Atmospherium Planetarium 60
Fleischmann, Max 60
Floyd, Pretty Boy 39, 40
Frémont, John C. 8–9
Frisch, Roy 39–40
Fuller, Charles W. 10
Fuller's Crossing 10, 25
Fuller's Folly 10

Gable, Clark 65–66
Garner, John Nance 71
Gates, Charles 10
Ginocchio, Andrew 116
Goddard, Paulette 52
Goff, Bruce 123
Gold Canyon 21–22, 24
Gold Hill 21, 24–26
Gold Hill Daily News 15
Gold Hill Mining District 33
Gold Hill News 61
Goldfield 35, 77
Goldwyn, Sam 63–64
Goodman, Joe 19
Gorrell, Robert 65

Graham, Bill 39–41, 43
The Granada 63
Great Basin 9, 33
Great Depression 43, 118
Grosch, Ethan and Hosea 21–23
Gunn, Barbara 65

Hammond and Wilson's Theater 63
Harolds Club 85, 88–90, 92, 107, 109, 111, 115, 119
Harrah, Bill 69, 91–99, 108, 109, 111–113
Harrah, John 92–95
Harrah's Club 5, 66, 68, 91, 96–99, 113, 115, 120
Harris, Len 104
Harrison, B. A. 25
Hastings, Lansford 9
Heart of Reno Chapel 56
Homestead Act 13
Hopkins, Mark 13
Hotel-casinos 113, 120, 123
Howard Theater 62
Howard, William Henry 62
Hughes, Howard 89, 111–112
Huntington, Collis P. 13, 75
Huston, John 65
Hyde, Orson 43

I Want to Quit Winners 87
Indians 6–8, 33, 113
International Hotel 30

James, Will 38
Jeffries, Jim 33, 36–37
Johnson, Jack 33, 36–37
Johnson, Lyndon B. 83
Johnson-Jeffries fight 35–38, 79, 116
Johntown 21

Kennedy, John F. 83

Kerkorian, Kirk 113
King, Henry 63–64
King, Thomas Starr 29
Kofoed, Leslie 89, 90, 107, 108

Lake House 13
Lake Mansion 12
Lake, Myron C. 10–15, 17, 113, 123
Lake's Crossing 11–13, 15, 123
Langan, Frank P. 49
Las Vegas 54
Last Chance 22
Last Frontier Hotel 54
Lawton Hot Springs 52
Laxalt, Joyce (Nielsen) 65
Laxalt, Robert 27, 35, 83
Lerude, Warren 50, 121
Lincoln, Abraham 11, 12, 13
Lincoln and Victory Highways 117
Luce, Henry 46
Lunsford, Ted 56

Maestretti, A. J. 53
Maguire, Tom 62
Maguire's Opera House 61–62
Maheu, Robert 111
Majestic Theater 63
Marion Rangers 19
Marriage laws 49, 54
Martin, Anne 81
McCarran, Pat 80
McClellan, Cyrennius 11
McCloskey, John R. 82
McKay, Jim 39, 40, 41, 43
McKissick Opera House 63
McKnight, William 53
McLaughlin, Patrick 24
Melcher, Venila and Joe 54–55, 56–57
Melton, Marilyn (Royle) 65
Melton, Rollan 56

Menken, Adah Isaacs 61
Merriman, Marion 50
MGM Grand 55
Miller, Arthur 65
Miller, Thomas W. 78
Mills, D. O. 72
Miscegenation Society 30
Monroe, Marilyn 65–67
Moore, Owen 49
Mormons 21, 43
Moseley, John O. 64, 65
Mount Davidson 16, 19, 21
Mouse game 88–89
Movie stars 64–67

National Bowling Stadium 123–124
Native Americans 6. Also see Indians
Nelson, Baby Face 39, 40
Neon 119
Nevada: immigrants 27; statehood 27
Nevada Historical Society 116
Nevada State Journal 36, 38, 46, 50, 66
Nevada State University 36
Nevada Territorial Legislature 33
Nevada Territory Bill 12
Nevada: The Last Frontier 59
Nevada Writers' Hall of Fame 38
Newlands, Francis G. 76–77
Newlands Reclamation Act 76
Nixon, George S. 63, 77
Nixon, Richard M. 83
Northern Mystery 7
Nye, J. W. 12, 33

Oddie, Tasker 77–78
Ophir 24–26
O'Riley, Peter 24
Overland Monthly 29

Paiute Indians 6–8, 113
Palace Club 91, 106
Palace Hotel 5
Palmer, Louise 29–30
Park Wedding Chapel 55–56
Petricianni, Silvio 91, 106, 108, 110
Pickford, Mary 49
Piper, John 62
Piper's Opera House 30–31, 62–63
Pittman, Key 71, 78–81
Pony Express 10–11, 13
Primadonna 100, 102–103, 120
Primm, Ernest 102–106
Pyramid Lake 8, 51–52, 67

Ralston, William 71–73
Reagan, Ronald 83
Red line 101–106
Reed, Virginia 10
Reno Anti-Gambling League 36
Reno Arch 115–119, 121–122
Reno Evening Gazette 53, 104
Reno Gazette-Journal 37, 115, 119, 122
Reno, Jesse Lee 15
Reno National Bank 40
Reno Pace 39
Reno Philharmonic 125
Reno Redevelopment Agency 122
Reno Rodeo 125
Reno Roundup Association 116
Reno World 123
RENOvation, Inc. 120
RenoVision 123
The Rialto 63
Riverside Bank 39
Riverside Hotel 40, 51, 55, 120, 123

Roberts, E. E. 42–43, 49, 116
Rocky Mountain Fur Company 7
Roosevelt, Franklin D. 71, 79
Roughing It 20, 28, 81
Route 66 67
Russell, Bertrand 47
Russell, John 47

Salmon Trout River 8
San Francisco 72, 73
Sanford, Leland 13
Schnitzer, William 48
Scott, Mabel 47
Scripps, E. W. 60
Senate Foreign Relations Committee 79
Sharon, Billy 74
Sharon, William 30, 71–76
Shoshone Indians 6
Sinatra, Frank 67
Six-Mile Canyon 24
Smith, Harold 86–90, 96
Smith, Jedediah 7–8
Smith, Raymond I. 85–92, 99, 109, 123, 125
Smith, Raymond, Jr. 87
Smith's Academy of Music 63
Somerville, Mollie Cooke 47
Sparks 78
Stack, Jim 60
Starlite Chapel 56
Stewart, William M. 74–75
Stockade 40–41
Stokowski, Leopold 50–51
Stone, John F. 10, 25
Storey County 74
Sullivan, Jack 91
Superstars 68
Sutro, Adolph 75–76
Sutro Tunnel 75
Sutter's Fort 9

Territorial Enterprise 12, 19, 20, 27, 28, 30, 61, 81

Territory of Nevada 12, 14,
  22, 27, 33
The Greatest Story Ever Told
  67
The Misfits 65–67
The Winning of Barbara Worth
  64
Theaters 62, 63
Tobin, Phil 42
Tonopah 35, 77
Transcontinental Highway
  Exposition 116
Transcontinental Railroad
  13
Truckee Meadows 9, 10, 12,
  13, 17, 25
Truckee River 6, 8, 10, 11,
  16, 28, 31, 115, 119, 120,
  122
Truckee River Walk 123
Twain, Mark 20, 28, 30–31,
  61, 81–82. *Also see* Samuel
  Clemens

U.S. Senate 74, 76–78
Union Pacific Company 13
University of Nevada 36, 38,
  60, 64–65, 124
Utah Territory 11, 27

Vanderbilt, Cornelius, III 60
Vanderbilt, Gloria 50–51
VanderMark, Jay 108
Virginia and Truckee
  Railroad 15–17, 30, 72
Virginia City 12–13, 17, 19,
  20, 25–31, 61–63, 72, 75

Walsh, James 25–26
Warren, Earl 87
Washoe County 25, 49, 53
Washoe County Court
  House 45, 54
Washoe Indians 6
Washoe Pines 52

Wedding chapels 55–56
West, Neil 51
Wheelman's Theater 63
Wilson, Tom 92
Wingfield, George 40, 77–78
Winnemucca 77
Woodward, Joseph 25
World War I 63
World War II 53, 89, 97, 98
Wright, William 20

Yerington, H. M. 71, 75

PICTURE CREDITS

Jean Dixon Aikin: 124

Lloyd Boles: 39

Don Dondero: 4, 66, 67, 83,
84, 86, 87, 88, 89, 100, 117

Harrah's: 44, 69, 91, 94, 97,
107, 114

Nevada Historical Society:
6, 7, 8, 9, 10, 11, 13, 14,
17, 18, 20, 21, 22, 23, 26,
29, 36, 37, 47, 48, 49, 63,
72, 73, 75, 76, 78, and
cover photo

Nevada Museum of Art: 125

Stanley Paher: 18

Park Wedding Chapel: 55

Reno Convention & Visitors
Authority News Bureau:
Cover insets, 30, 31, 58, 93

Reno Gazette-Journal: 103,
112, 119, 122

Craig Sailor: 123

University of Nevada, Reno,
Library–Special Collections
Department: 12, 25, 32, 35,
38, 51, 61, 70